FOLLOW THROUGH

TEACHERS' MANUAL

Jack Lonergan

Author's acknowledgements

Many ideas and suggestions from friends have been used in this
Teachers' Manual and accompanying Students' Book. I would
particularly like to acknowledge the contributions from Ken
Wilson (English Teaching Theatre) and Kathy Flower (BBC
English by Television), the constructive criticism of Ken Cripwell
and Chris Brumfit (University of London), the editorial skills of
Rosie Allen (BBC English by Television), and the development of
the audio materials by Geth Evans.

Book design: Peter McClure
Cover design: Jim Wire
Cover photography: Bay Hippisley

Printed and bound by Eyre & Spottiswoode
at Grosvenor Press Portsmouth

ISBN 0 946675 25 2

Contents

Introduction

FOLLOW THROUGH is a multi-media course for students who have completed a beginners' course in English (such as the BBC course FOLLOW ME). The course assumes a knowledge of English which approximately corresponds to the Council of Europe Threshold Level.

The course materials present English in a wide variety of communicative situations, and are designed to develop the students' fluency in speech and writing, as well as their listening and reading comprehension skills.

The FOLLOW THROUGH course consists of:
- 15 × 25 minute video units (or broadcast television programmes)
- 2 × C60 audiocassettes
- a book of the video scripts with detailed notes on language and subject matter
- a Students' Book
- this Teachers' Manual.

COURSE MATERIALS

VIDEO SERIES

The 15 video units are linked thematically. Each unit consists of:

Sit Com

The Sit Com features entertaining incidents in the lives of several people who work on a television programme called FOLLOW THROUGH. The people in these scenes speak at normal conversational speed but their vocabulary and grammar are carefully controlled. These scenes are used to present the major language topics.

Documentaries

Three of the people in the FOLLOW THROUGH scenes are reporters who make television documentaries about a variety of literary, cultural and recreational aspects of British life. Each documentary is a complete item, lasting three or four minutes. There are two documentaries in each unit (only one in Unit 15). The documentaries include interviews with people whose language is not controlled, and many of the people interviewed speak with regional British accents which the students may sometimes find quite difficult to understand. The aim of the documentaries is to give students the opportunity to listen to natural language used in authentic situations.

Conundrum

This is a murder mystery story and each unit includes a five-minute episode from it.

'Conundrum' is similar to any serial which might be seen on British television and the story is quite complicated. However, the episodes are short and the language is not too difficult to understand. It includes examples of the language points presented in the Sit Com scenes.

In Episode 1 the body of a murdered man is discovered in a hotel. The students follow the police investigations as they try to track down the murderer. A complex plot leads to the eventual revelation of the murderer's identity in Unit 15. Remember to keep the secret of 'Conundrum' from the students until they have watched all the episodes.

AUDIOCASSETTES

The two C60 audiocassettes consist of a variety of exercises which complement or extend the exercises in the Students' Book and provide extensive work on listening comprehension, oral production drills, pronunciation and intonation practice. They can be used either in the classroom or in a language laboratory. The symbol ⊙⊙ in this book indicates where there is an audio-related exercise.

The audio scripts are given at the back of this book.

VIDEO SCRIPTS

There is a separate book of video scripts containing the complete scripts of the video units with notes that explain colloquial, difficult or unusual words, expressions and other language points. There are also notes on subject matter which give background information on items or events referred to in the video.

If you have the scripts, you will find them very useful when planning the class, particularly if access to a video player is restricted outside classroom hours. Use them to make a note of the counter numbers on the video so you can find each sequence quickly and easily when you are taking the class, and also to mark any other language points or features you would like to highlight, for detailed study of individual utterances or sequences and for checking students' answers. (See p 6 for more detailed suggestions on preparation and the video scripts.)

STUDENTS' BOOK

The Students' Book reflects the composition of the video units. Each book unit is divided into three main sections – Sit Com, Documentaries, Conundrum – followed by a Language Study section.

Sit Com

The Students' Book material for each episode of the Sit Com is designed to help students understand what happens on the video, and to focus their attention on various aspects of communication, such as appropriacy of language in different situations, gestures and behaviour, as well as language functions.

Documentaries

The exploitation of the documentaries is different in style and approach. There is a written summary of the documentary, with some language practice and extension activities. These exercises are designed to complement the video presentation of the documentaries. Students can enjoy the experience of watching a short film about Britain, and use the printed material for preparation, later reference and project work.

Conundrum

To follow a murder mystery story in a foreign language means understanding the essential details of the plot. The Students' Book materials are designed to facilitate the students' understanding of the mystery, without destroying the tension and excitement of the puzzling murder story.

Language study

At the end of each unit, there is a Language Study section which concentrates on the major language points and other language points that occur in the unit. It draws on examples from the video sequences, and uses them to give the students an insight into different features of the English language. The Language Study section includes a Language Review which summarises the language points taught in the unit, and a glossary of Key Words and Phrases.

TEACHERS' MANUAL

This Teachers' Manual includes a general introduction on **Teaching with video,** which is intended to be a practical guide to the use of video in the classroom, with notes on some different approaches which can be used when teaching FOLLOW THROUGH. The general introduction is followed by detailed teaching notes and answers for all the exercises in the Students' Book. Suggestions are also made for further exploitation of some exercises, for project work and for follow-up activities.

TEACHING WITH VIDEO

Video is an extremely rich medium and it offers students a wide variety of visual experiences, as well as a great range of language. For many students this can be bewildering. You, as teacher, are there to select, recommend, prepare, re-use and follow up the contents of the FOLLOW THROUGH sequences. You can also guide the students in their learning techniques and strategies. The aim of this introduction is to help you to do that effectively.

1 PREPARATION

Preparation is, of course, an essential when teaching with video as with any other aid. Ideally, you should view every video sequence completely before using it in class. If you have the video scripts, read them carefully and mark items of interest. These may be language features: special vocabulary, important structures, idioms, colloquial language. Or they may be things like the physical background, people, places, clothes, behaviour, gestures, road signs, and so on. Alternatively, make a list of points as you watch the video. The Students' Book and this Teachers' Manual, of course, serve as the main guides to the key items of interest.

You may find that timetable difficulties or organisational problems such as room allocations or the availability of the video player make it impossible to view the whole sequence before you take the class. In this case, your main aids for preparation are the video scripts, if you have them, and the Students' Book. It must be emphasised that this is a less satisfactory solution that loses many of the benefits of more detailed preparation, which comes only when you *watch* the whole video sequence. For example, the important gestures and signals made by the characters, the intonation in their voices or the background music and sound effects all add considerably to the richness of video sequences as a teaching resource.

Finding the right place on a videocassette is important. If the video player has a counter, then return the counter to 000 at the beginning of the cassette and note the counter numbers at the beginning of the sequences and of items you want to point out so that you can find them again quickly and easily.

2 ORGANISATION IN THE CLASSROOM

The layout of the classroom varies greatly both within institutions and throughout the world. You may not have direct control over the physical teaching situation. Students may sit at fixed benches or tables; they may be in rows, pairs or circular groups; they may just sit on the floor. Whatever the situation, it is essential that *all* the students can see the television screen clearly.

A class of thirty students should be able to see well enough if they group themselves around the screen. If necessary, some students can sit in the aisles or gangways during a viewing. For very large classes, for example, in a full lecture hall, it is useful – if luxurious – to have more than one television screen placed around the room.

When you are showing FOLLOW THROUGH, the focus of attention should be the television screen. The television set should stand alone, with you to the side, or among or behind the students. Ideally, use a remote control facility to operate the video player. If this is not available, then long cables can be used between the video player and the television screen, so that the person operating the video player does not obstruct vision of the screen.

Other classroom aids may distract attention, so overhead projectors, for example, should be switched off or removed before the television is switched on. Care should also be taken that there are no annoying reflections of sunlight or classroom lighting on the screen.

3 ACTIVE VIEWING

Domestic television is so closely associated with entertainment and relaxation that many students watching video in the classroom may expect only to be entertained. It is therefore essential that students appreciate how valuable the video can be for learning as well as for entertainment.

The FOLLOW THROUGH materials aim to encourage students to view actively, to respond to the video so that they can gain more from their viewing. To achieve this, the students' attention is focused on certain parts of each video sequence. This helps ensure comprehension as well as increasing their enjoyment and satisfaction in viewing. In addition, active viewing maintains the students' motivation. The practical teaching suggestions in this Teachers' Manual are all designed to encourage active participation by the students.

Working with FOLLOW THROUGH on video does not mean that you have to adopt a completely new methodology. You will recognise familiar teaching techniques in many of the detailed suggestions in the Students' Book and this Teachers' Manual. If you use wallcharts, magazine pictures, blackboard drawings, or group work activities, then you can apply your own successful teaching methods to video, making adaptations as necessary. Of course, the special nature of video (sound and vision that can be held or repeated at any time) means that there will be some classroom techniques that are really unique to video. But even these draw on established teaching ideas for their proven effectiveness.

4 PRACTICAL TEACHING SUGGESTIONS

Most language learners are quite used to television – but not in the classroom. They expect television to be a one-way medium from television to viewer. These suggestions show how you can encourage the students to interact with the video sequences. All the facilities of the video player should be used: freeze-frame, replay, playing without sound, playing without vision and so on. Details of these facilities are given on page 16.

The ideas outlined here concentrate on different aspects of language teaching and the use of video. You can freely adapt any of these ideas for use with different levels of language students. Once you have tried out these suggestions, you may wish to develop further ideas of your own.

   i) Active viewing guides
  ii) Silent sequences
 iii) Video with no picture
 iv) Non-verbal signals
  v) Recall and narration
 vi) Speculation
 vii) Register and appropriacy
viii) Vocabulary development and structure practice
 ix) Transfer activities
  x) Information gaps

i) Active viewing guides

To follow a dialogue, narrative or commentary in English that may be difficult, students need to have a general understanding of what they will see and hear. Active viewing guides are simple comprehension tasks that focus on the essential information and action in a video sequence. Their main purpose is to increase the students' understanding – not to test them. The tasks are designed to be easy to complete, and require students simply to make a tick or a cross in a series of boxes. These viewing guides help students follow the video sequence, and often give them the satisfaction of discovering key information for themselves. This is motivating, reinforcing the attractions of television and encourages students to be alert, active viewers.

The active viewing guides in FOLLOW THROUGH serve several purposes. Some establish who characters are and the relationships between them, some draw attention to key language items, while others focus on aspects of communication such as gestures and facial expressions. The following viewing guide is from the Sit Com in Unit 4.

3 Travellers

Where have the FOLLOW THROUGH staff been to abroad? Tick (√) the places they have been.

	Billy	Sarah	Joe
Italy			
North Africa			
nowhere			
the Middle East			
Tenerife			

The task is easy, it is designed for success, but it is easy only if the destinations are known to the students. It could be too much to expect some students to pick up the names of the countries without preparation.

A similar type of guide is one that includes more information than is necessary: This guide is from the Sit Com in Unit 5.

2 Julie's mother

Julie's mother has a lot of curios and bric-a-brac. Check that you know the following, and tick (√) the ones that you see in the living room.

☐ a cakestand   ☐ an Italian wine bottle

☐ a blazing fire   ☐ a grand piano

☐ a tapestry wall hanging   ☐ a sun goddess

☐ a standard lamp   ☐ a grandfather clock

☐ Spanish dancers   ☐ a portrait of Julie's father

☐ a temple dancer from Burma   ☐ a photograph of Julie's father

This is basically a vocabulary extension activity. By introducing *possibilities,* the students' search is like a detective game; more stimulating, and therefore more useful, than just learning vocabulary lists.

Understanding a video sequence sometimes depends on understanding a particular item of essential information. This is especially true of the murder mystery serial 'Conundrum'. In order to appreciate how the mystery is solved, it is essential that the students follow the plot and notice the relevant points. However, the drama in the story should not be spoiled by making the points too obvious.

The following viewing guide from Unit 1 focuses on the characters of the hotel manager and Michael Kelly, the waiter who found the body of the murdered man. The guide not only heightens the students' interest in two of the suspects, but it also increases their vocabulary to describe people.

2 The hotel staff

The manager meets Michael Kelly, a hotel waiter, outside the service lift. Which words describe them?

	Michael Kelly	the manager
well-dressed		
scruffy		
hard-working		
trustworthy		
dishonest		
friendly		
arrogant		

Explain your opinions and reasons to two other students in your class. Try to agree on a list of characteristics for the waiter and the manager. Write a short description of their characters.

Sometimes a sequence can be understood by most of the students, but you will want to draw attention to key features in the language. The following example from Unit 3 illustrates this.

1 Exaggeration

Everyone at the FOLLOW THROUGH office exaggerates. Who says the following things? Write the names in the left-hand column. If you think what they say is true, put a tick (√) in the right-hand column. If you think it is an exaggeration, put a cross (×).

Who says . . .?		. . . is it true?
	When you learn to pay your debts, I'll learn how to make a good cup of tea.	
	The next time someone shouts at me, I'll tell them to wait until I'm ready.	
	If I'm caught, I'll be put in prison for hundreds of years.	
	Don't worry, Billy. I'll visit you every twenty-five years!	
	I'll have to sell that car. It's more trouble than it's worth.	
	Sarah's going to find the second-best clairvoyant in Europe. Today. Somewhere in London.	

Explain your reasons to other people in your class.

This viewing guide can be treated in two stages. Firstly, the students are guided to listen to who says what in the dialogue. This task requires just one-word answers. Secondly, the students are asked to listen and interpret the degree of truth in what is said. You will probably need to stop the videocassette at selected points to allow the students time to write their answers. Depending on the level of ability of the students, the videocassette should be played (with pauses) once, twice or even more times.

Integrating viewing guides into the lesson

The aim of the viewing guide is to aid comprehension. Watching FOLLOW THROUGH on video motivates students and the guides are designed to build on this positive feature. Do not use the guides to catch students out – which will demoralise them – by asking them to complete them without proper preparation.

There are three clear stages for using viewing guides:
- pre-teaching the aims and the language of the guide
- watching the video and completing the task
- follow-up activities.

The language in the viewing guide should first be prepared thoroughly with the students. Next, the viewing guide should be completed while or immediately after watching the video. With most guides, the students can note their answers while viewing the sequence for the first time. With others, the sequence may have to be played twice or more before they can complete the task.

With some guides, especially when note-taking is required, the sequence may have to be interrupted and paused. This is to allow time for thinking and writing. Students cannot be expected to write and watch at the same time.

When completed, the viewing guides are useful to students as reference notes for information about the various FOLLOW THROUGH sequences. They can be used for immediate feedback as soon as the task is completed: ask comprehension questions based on the viewing guide to check that everyone has understood the sequence. This gives students the opportunity to talk in class and to practise speaking from notes or outlines. The viewing guides are also useful later. Several days after watching the video sequence, you might want to revise the content of the sequence. The completed viewing guide serves as an excellent memory aid for the students. When they look at the guide, two motivating factors are apparent:

- the students are reading from their own (correct) notes
- the viewing guide draws the attention of the whole class together, reminding them of the shared experience of watching the video.

ii) Silent sequences

Watching FOLLOW THROUGH can often be made even more intriguing by playing the videocassette with the sound turned off. These silent sequences provide excellent opportunities for practice in narrating or describing what has happened or what is happening at the moment. (Note that the sound adjustment control is normally on the television set, and not on the video player.) The following viewing task from the Sit Com in Unit 7 requires little more than observation, once the language in the guide is understood.

1   In the office

Billy wants to change his lifestyle to keep fit.
What can you see that shows that he has
tried? Tick (√) what he does.

A He arrives for work early. ☐
B He is wearing a tracksuit. ☐
C He is wearing running shorts. ☐
D He eats fresh apples. ☐
E He drinks fresh orange juice. ☐
F He does physical exercises. ☐
G He jogs around the office. ☐

The next viewing task, from the same unit, requires different language skills. The guide structures the account which the students must give either orally, or in writing.

2   In the canteen

Sarah has difficulty in making a cup of instant coffee. Write an account of what happened, using the following words and phrases.

first of all...	opened	instant coffee
so...	put...in	a coffee tin
then...	took...out	a lid
because...	looked at	sugar
as...	turned...round	a spoon
and finally...	saw that it was	a spoonful of
	poured...back	a cup
	was labelled	

iii) Video with no picture

A variation is to play the video with the sound on, but with no picture. Turn the contrast control on the television set to very dark, so that the screen remains blank or simply turn the television around so the students cannot see the screen. Play the videocassette as a soundtrack only. Proceed with comprehension work on the soundtrack until you are sure the students understand the language they have heard. Then get the students to prepare a description of what they imagine the pictures show at each point, where the characters might be, what they are doing, the expressions on their faces, etc.

iv) Non-verbal signals

Using video for language teaching allows you to focus attention on some of the most important features of communication. Non-verbal information, conveyed by facial expressions, gestures, movements of the body and so on, communicate a great deal of any message. All students who are going to meet native speakers of English need to recognise these aspects of communication. For many students they present a model which must be imitated and mastered.

A simple way of focusing the students' attention on such features is to offer a choice. The students will probably need to be taught some of the vocabulary in advance, as the language used to describe behaviour is different from the spoken language in the FOLLOW THROUGH scenes. Students need to be prepared so that they are able and willing to voice their interpretations. Here is an example from the Sit Com in Unit 4. Students can also mime the emotions and reactions listed in a role play activity.

1 At the travel agent's

What words would you use to describe Billy and the travel agent?
Tick (√) the words you choose.

Billy		travel agent
	annoyed	
	curious	
	eager	
	embarrassed	
	helpful	
	interested	
	pleased	
	surprised	

v) Recall and narration

You can interrupt any video sequence at almost any point to provide an opportunity for the students to retell what they have just seen. This type of activity gives practice in the language features used in story-telling and recall, for example, the use of the past simple and past continuous tenses, the use of connectors, and so on. In this example from the Sit Com in Unit 4, the students must provide the connectors.

2 Car thief

Retell the story of the car theft. Use the
following words and phrases.
A . . . went into the office
B . . . drove away
C . . . stopped
D . . . was struggling with the car door
E . . . came round the corner
F . . . opened the door
G . . . was trying to open it
H . . . watched what was happening
I . . . shrugged
J . . . got in

Stopping the cassette and asking questions is very easy to do with video. It can have great benefits, but remember that there is little point in asking the class questions which require language in the answers which is more difficult than the language you are teaching. This is particularly true if the students are asked to speculate, or to interpret what they see.

vi) Speculation

Inviting students to speak is valuable because it allows them freedom to use the language that they know. On some video players, you can hold a picture on the screen by using the 'freeze' button. In 'Conundrum', speculation is an essential part of the story, as the students are often invited to discuss what happens next. Here is an example from Unit 4.

3 Discussion

The hotel manager listens at the door as
Detective Constable Maxwell interviews
Kelly. What is the manager trying to do?
What do you think Kelly can tell us about
him?

Speculation activities can also be used in group work for writing possible endings to sequences. Stop the videocassette and ask the students what will happen next. Students can work in small groups, scripting possible continuation sequences. These can be read or acted out to the class, and then the class can vote on different groups' ideas. When this has been done there will be the interest (and amusement) in seeing the FOLLOW THROUGH version.

vii) Register and appropriacy

FOLLOW THROUGH presents a language in a context. The full communicative situation can be appreciated by the students because they are provided with a large amount of visual detail about the speakers and the setting. Video helps students understand the differences in formal and informal language, polite and impolite language, degrees of anger, enjoyment, liking, disliking and so on. Even students who have attained a fairly good standard of English may find it difficult to choose appropriate language to suit different situations.

This extract from Unit 5 shows how students can be made familiar with differing language registers and their appropriacy in different situations.

4 Flashback

Hutchinson explains to the police how he met Alec Lee in the hotel bar, when he was having a drink with Gibbs. Watch the flashback sequence carefully, and then look at the dialogue possibilities below. What do you think they said? Remember they are professional colleagues meeting in a bar.

Write **A**, **B** or **C** in each box on the left to show what each person says.

		A	B	C
	Gibbs:	Ah, Alec. Good evening!	Ah, good evening Mr Lee. How very nice of you to come!	Alec, hello!
	Lee:	Mr Gibbs, may I say it really is a pleasure to be here.	Hi! Everything okay?	Good evening, Matthew. And how are you?
	Gibbs:	Come and sit down.	Come over here and sit down.	Do please take a seat.
	Hutchinson:	Sit here.	Here, have my seat. I'm just going.	I'm leaving actually. Do take my seat.
	Lee:	Thank you very much indeed. That really is most kind of you.	Thanks.	Thank you very much.

This is an important exercise for many students, as they often lack experience of using their English in a variety of different social situations. For this reason, the errors that they make may be insignificant in terms of grammar or vocabulary, but may be significant in terms of appropriacy. That is, without intending to be, they sound over-polite, too brusque or not as enthusiastic as they wish to be.

You can extend this idea by asking the students to provide alternatives to what they hear, but which match what they see. With good classes most of the suggestions will be grammatically correct, but some suggestions may be inappropriate; they may be too impolite or too formal, or they may be expressed in language more usually used with a different social group, such as children.

viii) Vocabulary development and structure practice

FOLLOW THROUGH presents students with an almost limitless visual resource, equivalent to many thousands of magazine pictures. Any picture or sequence can be used for vocabulary building and structure practice.

This is particularly true of the documentary sequences. These give students an insight into diverse areas of life in the UK.

The richness of the visual information in FOLLOW THROUGH may well prompt students to ask questions about what they see. At all levels of language competence and social sophistication, there will be students who will see on the screen things that interest, puzzle, surprise or annoy them. You should let the students have some autonomy. Build into some lessons a session in which they can call out whenever they want you to stop the videocassette. They can then ask questions about what they have seen or heard. This procedure has two advantages:

firstly, it provides a genuine environment for questions initiated by the class because the motivation and interest shown are the students' own. Secondly, the question might spark off the possibility for structure practice or some other follow-up teaching/learning phase. Students are always more receptive to teaching if it is in response to their own expressed interests.

ix) Transfer activities

The need for active viewing and classroom techniques which encourage interaction between student and video underlies all the activities in the Students' Book. It is also important to develop language activities which extend the material presented by the video sequences into the realm of the students' own interests and experiences.

Examples of this are the discussion activities based on the documentaries. The video sequence (and the audio and book material) provide the stimulus. The students follow this up in their own way.

Role play is an excellent way of practising speaking. It also helps to overcome the reluctance of many students to speak freely, often caused by their fear of making mistakes. Role plays can be based on the situations presented on the video but they allow students to vary the language used.

As we have seen above, communication is more than just words; it is behaviour too. The way we use our hands and arms, our facial expressions, the way we sit and stand, the distance we put between one another when we speak – these can all be observed on video and practised in role play. Good role playing is more than just reading a part in a dialogue; it is assuming the role of another person and talking and behaving accordingly. Students therefore should be encouraged to get up, walk around and act the role they are taking. FOLLOW THROUGH provides the model and shows how native speakers actually behave when speaking. Encourage your students to copy. They will be more effective communicators in English if they do.

If you have the book of FOLLOW THROUGH video scripts, they can always be used for reference and for students to act out scenes in the classroom. This is especially useful in the early stages of role playing.

x) Information gaps

An effective way of setting up a situation in which the students can communicate what they see in FOLLOW THROUGH is to create an information gap. This means giving information to some of the students in the class but withholding it from the others.

One technique for organising this is to divide the class into pairs: Student **A** and Student **B**. All the **A**s sit with their backs to the screen. At the same time the **B**s watch a silent sequence. At the end of the sequence, each Student **A** must ask Student **B** questions to discover what happened.

A variation on this approach is to create a complete video split; that is, the sound and the vision are presented separately to the class divided into two groups. Students **A** watch a silent sequence and then write a possible video script. Students **B** either listen to the video without the picture or read the actual video script (with stage instructions deleted) if you have it and anticipate what is happening on the screen. In pairs, **A**s and **B**s then compare notes and discuss the differences. Piecing together what happened and what was said is now slightly more difficult as both Students **A** and Students **B** in each pair will need to ask and answer detailed questions.

Whichever technique is used, the communicative task is the same: the students pool their knowledge and through communicating with each other fill in the gaps in their knowledge.

5   FACILITIES ON THE VIDEO PLAYER

The outstanding point about modern video players is the ease and simplicity of their use. Most video players are designed for use in the home. This means that the range of facilities the video player has is determined by requirements of domestic use. However, these facilities can easily be adopted for use with a class.

Basic functions on video players

All video recorders have the following functions:

START	and	STOP

The cassette can be stopped or started at any place; there is no need to rewind to the beginning.

REWIND	and	FORWARD WIND

No picture is seen nor sound heard when this facility is used. The cassettes wind forwards and backwards at great speed.

Most video players have the following functions:

PAUSE

This halts the cassette while leaving it ready for immediate play. On many machines this function switches itself off after two minutes. When the cassette is paused, there is no picture on the screen.

FREEZE

This is a pause button with the added advantage of 'freezing' the image on the television screen. This facility is a very useful function for language teaching. You can exploit the content of the screen pictures in the same way as you would a flash card or magazine picture. However, the screen image is not so clear when this function is used.

COUNTER

Most video players have counters which revolve from 000 to 999. Note the counter numbers to mark points of interest and to prepare for lessons.

Some video recorders also have the following functions:

PICTURE SEARCH

The cassette can be wound forward or backward rapidly with a fast moving picture visible. This is extremely useful for finding particular scenes on a video.

REMOTE CONTROL

With a remote control facility, the teacher can move away from the video player to be among the students. Some remote control units are linked to the player by a cable. This is satisfactory, but an infra-red control unit is far better for it has no physical link to the television set or player and it allows all the functions on the player to be controlled from anywhere in the classroom.

UNIT 1

Hello!

Greeting people

AIMS The main aim of this first unit is to present FOLLOW THROUGH to the students:

– introducing the characters in the situation comedy (Sit Com)

– introducing the students to the documentary films (Doc Spots)

– establishing the plot of 'Conundrum'

– familiarising the students with the types of activities included in the course

The language focus in this unit is on greetings and descriptions.

For some students, the exercises on greetings may be easy, but they may also be a first introduction to the concept of register. It is important that the students appreciate how language used to communicate one idea can change if circumstances change. This involves the roles of the speakers – their age, sex and status – as well as where the dialogue takes place. The exercises on description and the order of adjectives are intended to revise and consolidate the students' present ability to use English.

PRE-VIEWING PREPARATION

SIT COM: **1 Who's who in FOLLOW THROUGH?**
5 In the restaurant

DOC SPOTS: **Cross-Channel ferries** reading passage and **1 Comprehension**
Publishing reading passage and **1 Comprehension**

CONUNDRUM: **The language of murder**

LANGUAGE REVIEW

In this unit you have practised

1 greeting people formally and informally:
How do you do. Hello. Hi!

2 describing people:
Corinne finds plants more interesting than people.
Mrs Belmont usually wears a green overall and brown trousers.

3 describing things and places:
Crossing the Channel by train and boat is quite cheap and very relaxing.

4 combining several adjectives in one phrase:
a nice American guy
a giant long-tailed ferry-eating monster

KEY WORDS AND PHRASES

adverse
to afford
an airline
artistic
a best seller
a boss
a cafeteria
a crew
delicious
a detective
efficient
to exaggerate
expensive
a ferry
a fortune
a gale
a guy (colloquial)
a hairstyle
happy-go-lucky
a hazard
a holiday-maker
a hotel lobby
imagination
to insert
insurance
to make up one's mind
a message
a metaphor
nothing but
odd
an olive
original
a parking meter
a patron

PAYMENT
You can pay hotel bills
● by cheque
● by credit card
or you can pay by cash.

petrol
a philosopher
a plant
to plug in
a pop star
probably
to publish
to register
a registration card
to repair
repairs
road tax

SALADE NICOISE
A mixed salad with olives, anchovy fillets, tuna fish and hard boiled eggs.

a sandwich
smart
a staff canteen
to switch off
to switch on
talented

a television producer
to trace
a tramp

TRAVEL IN LONDON
You can travel around London by bus, by tube (Underground), by car or by taxi.

a uniform
unique
wallpaper

WORD PROCESSORS
A floppy disc is part of the software of a word processor: a data disc is one full of information. The discs are operated by the disc drive.

 SIT COM

1 Who's who in FOLLOW THROUGH?

This exercise establishes the main characters in the Sit Com.

Check that the students understand the vocabulary in the viewing guide before playing the scene for the first time. The viewing guide can be completed by students in various ways:

- let them discuss in small groups who is who, after one viewing
- let them complete the guide individually as they watch
- use the clues in the guide as cues for students to call out when they hear the identyfing phrase

The correct order for the answers is:
G, B, F, D, H, A, C, E

 1 Welcome to FOLLOW THROUGH

2 What are they wearing?

This exercise teaches the students some vocabulary of clothing, and introduces a variety of adjectives. The guide can be treated as a note-taking or memory exercise.

Draw the students' attention to compound adjectives such as *open-necked*. They may need a wider range of words for **3 Can you describe . . .?**, for example, *high-necked, fur-lined, silk-edged*.

The correct order for the answers is:
Prodip, Corinne, Ted Stenhouse, Joe, Mrs Belmont, Billy, Sarah

 2 Drill

3 Can you describe . . .?

This writing task can be used for homework or private study. Instead of describing members of the class, the students could choose to describe a person in a magazine, or even a popular television programme. Alternatively, the quiz can take place in a lesson *after* the observation; this makes the task more difficult, as students describe what their colleagues *were wearing* – they may have changed their clothes. This gives the opportunity to introduce the past tense forms *was . . . . ing* and *were . . . . ing* which will be covered in Unit 4.

4 In the office

This question focuses the students' attention on a joke that recurs in several episodes of the Sit Com. Ted Stenhouse always asks Corinne – in an angry way – why something has been done, and whose idea it was or who ordered it. The answer is always the same: 'Yours, Mr Stenhouse!' or 'You did, Mr Stenhouse!'.

5 In the restaurant

Prodip's visits to Pierre's restaurant are one of the recurring themes in the Sit Com.

This exercise presents to the students in written form the names of some European philosophers. If the class are not already familiar with the philosophers, then the task of identifying their nationalities can be used as an introduction to information retrieval skills. The sentence writing task can be used as homework.

The answers are:
Descartes, Rousseau, Sartre, Voltaire = French;
Kant, Nietzsche = German; Kierkegaard = Danish;
Erasmus = Dutch; Machiavelli = Italian;
Mill = British; Plato = Greek.

D◉ DOC SPOT 1   Cross-Channel ferries

1   Comprehension

Present the reading passage and comprehension questions as pre-viewing activities. When the students understand the topic and the essential vocabulary, play the Doc Spot.

The answers are:

A No, there are many other boats and ships.

B They are travelling to and from Northern Europe.

C a congested area, where all the traffic gathers to pass through a narrow stretch of sea

D a person who goes and comes back again on the same day

E the wind

F They listen to BBC weather reports four times a day and they get gale warnings.

3   Listen for detail

2   Writing

This task can be carried out individually, in pairs or in small groups. It is suitable for homework or class study.

Let groups act out the dialogue they have written.

3   Role play

This activity is a development of **2 Writing**. The students should move away from reading a prepared dialogue to speaking from cues, as given in the exercise. If this is too difficult for the students, let them prepare dialogues as in **2 Writing**, and then act them out, or move to role play in a later unit.

4   Travel and you

Provide the class with English language brochures about foreign places. You should be able to obtain these free from travel agents.

You could also prepare blank maps of foreign countries for the students to fill in in English: students can mark and label the international travel routes (roads, rail, sea and air routes, etc).

D◉ DOC SPOT 2   Publishing

1   Comprehension

Present the reading passage and comprehension questions as a pre-viewing exercise. When the students understand the topic and the key vocabulary, play the Doc Spot.

The answers are:

A new, previously unpublished books
B No, between 30,000 and 40,000 books are published in Britain alone.
C No, he likes something unusual or unconventional.
D A patron provides a writer or artist with money so that he or she can afford to practise his or her art.
E No, they do not always make the right choice.
F Conrad was Polish but he wrote 'immaculate' English.

2 Writing

This task can be used for homework or private study.

The answers are:

A There used to be very few televisions. Nowadays, every home has a television/has one.
B It used to take four days to fly to Australia. Nowadays, it (only) takes twenty hours.
C English fruit used to be cheap. Nowadays, it is expensive.
D The River Thames used to be dirty and polluted. Nowadays, it is full of fish.
E Football players used to be paid £20 a week. Nowadays, they are paid £1,000 a match.

3 English language authors

This activity extends the students' skills at retrieving information. If there is easy access to large numbers of books – a library, bookshop or local Anglophile – use the authors listed as a basis for a survey project. The students can be split into groups, and asked to find out the proportion of books stocked which are written by each author – for example, Shakespeare forms fifteen per cent of the local bookshop's stock.

The answers are:

crime fiction	Agatha Christie, Raymond Chandler
poetry	William Wordsworth, John Milton, (William Shakespeare also wrote many poems and sonnets)
science fiction	Ray Bradbury, Isaac Asimov
plays	Arthur Miller, William Shakespeare
comic novels	P G Wodehouse, Tom Sharpe

4 Famous Authors

The students can copy the puzzle from the book if they are not allowed to write in the book.

The puzzle can be used as a competition between small groups of students in class: which group can solve the puzzle first?

The answers are:

1) and 4) Joseph Conrad; 2) patron; 3) thriller; 5) and 7) Secker (and) Warburg; 6) unusual); 8) risks

The key word is 'hardback' – a book bound in hard covers.

5 Books and you

This activity can be extended to become a survey (in English) of what the students like to read in their own language(s), or the writing exercise can be used for homework.

 CONUNDRUM

The language of murder

Prepare for Episode 1 of 'Conundrum' with this exercise. Students need to know the English terms for the key elements of a police murder investigation.

The answers are:

A 2) **B** 5) **C** 4) **D** 3) **E** 1)

1 Who's who in CONUNDRUM?

This exercise establishes the identity of six of the characters in the murder mystery, apart from the investigating police officers. In Episode 2, the students will also meet the murdered man's widow, Mrs Gibbs, and the Gibbs' neighbour, Mrs Taylor.

The answers are: **A, C**

2 The hotel staff

This exercise focuses on the hotel manager and Michael Kelly. It also extends the students' ability to describe and talk about people. Note the further use of compound adjectives in the viewing guide: *well-dressed, hard-working.*

3 What happens next?

As 'Conundrum' is a murder mystery, there are two things essential for the students' enjoyment of the serial. Firstly, they must fully understand what has happened in each episode. Secondly, they must be kept in suspense until the last episode. Speculation tasks such as this help ensure that both things are happening.

This activity is suitable for homework, group work or individual study. The written answers can be compared orally in class in a subsequent lesson, before the next episode is shown.

  4 Who said it?

LANGUAGE STUDY

1 Hello!

Exchanging greetings, pleasantries and farewells varies greatly from culture to culture. The exercises here concentrate on modern idiomatic British English – as spoken by most of the characters seen on screen. Usage in American English – as spoken by Joe in the Sit Com – tends to be more informal than in British English. For example, Mr Stenhouse is almost always called by his title (Mr) and his last name (Stenhouse) by the staff below him. In some less traditional British companies, and in many American companies, he would be called by his first name (Ted). 'Ted' is an abbreviation of the christian name 'Edward'. Another popular form of address among business colleagues in the United States of America is to use initials only – so Mr Stenhouse would be 'ES'.

At a first introduction in British English, the normal rule is
- a full sentence to say who you are
- ellipsis to make a pleasantry

For example:

    I'm Ted Stenhouse.
            or   Pleased to meet you.
    My name's Stenhouse.

The answers to Exercise 1 are:

only once ever:	How do you do.
once a day:	Good morning/afternoon/evening!
	How are you?
two or three times a day:	Hello! Hi!

The answers to Exercise 2 are:

How do you do.	How do you do.
Good morning.	Morning. Hello. Hi.
Good afternoon.	Hi. Hello. ('Afternoon.' is another possible reply.)
Good evening.	Good evening. Hi. Hello.
How are you today?	Fine thanks. Not too bad.
	Very well, thank you.
	All right, thanks.
How are things?	Not too bad. All right, thanks. Fine thanks.
Hello./Hi.	Hello./Hi.
Hi, how's it going?	Fine thanks. Not too bad. All right, thanks.

  5 Pronunciation and intonation

2   Adjectives

This sentence illustrates the main rules for adjective order:
His first rare small blue Chinese porcelain drinking vessel.
Students could make up similar sentences.

In 'Conundrum', the hotel manager says to Kelly, the waiter, '*It gets pretty hot working here, doesn't it?*' using *pretty* as a modifying adverb in the sense of *fairly, quite.*

Adverbs used to modify adjectives do not disturb the word order rules, for example:
A tall, 65-year old man.
A very tall, young looking 65-year old man.

The answers to Exercise 3 are:

A There is one nice tall American television reporter on the FOLLOW THROUGH team.

B Sarah sometimes wears her brown leather boots and her new red velvet skirt.

C In CONUNDRUM, Detective Constable Maxwell has to investigate her first murder mystery.

D The cross-Channel ferry crews listen to regular BBC weather forecasts.

E Pierre is very proud of his popular French restaurant.

  6 Pronunciation

Encourage the students to use their imagination in Exercise 4. Introduce modifying adverbs into the students' sentences if that does not cause difficulty.

Students may need reminding that some adjectives are the same when used as adverbs, for example:
direct, early, hard, high, late, long, short, straight

These should not be confused with the following adverbs which have different meanings:
directly, hardly, highly, lately, shortly

UNIT 2

What will happen?

Talking about the future

AIMS

The main aid of this unit is to extend the students' ability to talk about the future. The theme of futurity is continued in Unit 3.

PRE-VIEWING PREPARATION

SIT COM: **1 The next bus**

Prepare vocabulary for **2 Corinne's plants** and **3 Zita Starlight's arrival.**

DOC SPOTS: **Hampton Court** reading passage and **1 Comprehension**
Making it big reading passage and **1 Comprehension**

CONUNDRUM: Check key vocabulary.

LANGUAGE REVIEW

In this unit you have practised

1 talking about natural events, timetables and forecasts using the 'will' future:
By the time spring comes, you'll be so healthy!
We'll never be ready on time!
The next bus will be here in four minutes.

2 expressing intentions using the 'going to' future:
I'm going to create a master tape.

3 talking about things which are certain to happen in the future using 'will':
By the time I get to the office, I will have missed my morning coffee.

4 expressing probability and likelihood using 'will probably', 'should have' and 'about to':
I'll probably have to work through the lunch hour.
You shouldn't have any problems.
I'm about to resign from this job.

5 expressing something less likely using 'I'd rather . . .':
I'd rather be a famous pop star.

25

KEY WORDS AND PHRASES

AT THE AIRPORT
Zita Starlight's plane arrives at Terminal Three. She won't go to the arrival hall, but to the VIP lounge (VIP = Very Important Person). There is also a departure lounge in the terminal building.

to be amazed
an autograph
a balcony
a barrier
to clean up
a commission
a corridor
to define
delightful
a description
a destination
to die
difficult
to employ
to be employed
an engineer
evidence
fame
a fan
to be fed up
a fingerprint
to be fond of
fresh
to get lost
glamorous
grateful
to guarantee
a guitarist
a highlight

to identify
an influence
an interview
to keep
a landscape gardener
a limousine

MEALS AND BREAKS
breakfast; breakfast-time TV;
morning coffee; coffee break;
lunch; lunch hour;
afternoon tea; teatime; tea break;
dinner; dinner time;
supper; supper time.

magnificent
a maze
a monarch
a murderer
naturally
a note
to notice
old-fashioned
a palace
a percentage
a pinstripe suit
to plant out
a poem
a programme

to recite
to recognise
to record
a registration number
to regret
regular
a residence
to resign
a rose
a stately home
a studio
to throw away
a tourist attraction
to trace
trouble
    to get into trouble
a vine
a violet
a window box

COMPOUND ADJECTIVES
middle-aged
high-heeled
knee-length
old-fashioned

CONVERSATION
In general: plants need love and conversation.
In particular: Corinne was told that during a conversation with the gardener.

PHRASES
Let's look on the bright side!

GUIDE TO THE UNIT

 SIT COM

1 The next bus

Successful completion of this task will ensure that the students have understood the bus inspector's joke.

Prepare the content of the viewing guide before showing the scene. If buses are used locally, then ask the class what reasons are usually given by staff when buses do not run. Be sure that the class understand the difference between *to tell a joke* (to tell a funny story), and *to joke,* or *to make a joke* (to behave in a funny way).

The answers are:

A true   **B** false   **C** false   **D** false   **E** true   **F** false

2 Corinne's plants

This guide helps students to follow the conversation between the gardener and Corinne. The main language focus in the guide is on expressions of time. Those listed here are varied: *in (+ noun)* referring to fixed times; *once a (+ noun)* and *all the (+ noun)* referring to repeated time.

The unit includes many other expressions of time which have no introductory word or phrase, for example: *tomorrow afternoon, this evening, any minute.*

Select suitable scenes from the Sit Com before you take the class and make a note of the counter numbers. Then replay these scenes to the students and get them to listen for and note down expressions of time.

Use the video and/or video script to check answers; explain any that prove difficult.

 1   Corinne's plants

3 Zita Starlight's arrival

This guide focuses on visual information and follows up the activities in Unit 1.

If necessary, Sit Com **3 Can you describe . . .?** in Unit 1 can be repeated or extended.

The answers are:

Mrs Belmont normally wears a headscarf, a pink cardigan and flat shoes.
For Zita Starlight she wears a flowery headband, knee-length trousers, a fancy waistcoat and high-heeled boots.

4 Roses are red

This type of verse which is not intended to be serious is known as *doggerel.* It is popular for humour in many English-speaking countries. One of its features is that it either breaks the conventions of verse quite bizarrely or, as in this case, the rhythm and beat are exaggeratedly strict. For this reason, doggerel is read in an emphatic manner; if students have difficulty with stress, then doggerel can be used deliberately for practice.

Here is another well-known example:

East is East, and West is West,
But I always say that home is best.

Get the class to compose some doggerel, working in small groups.

The missing words are:
be true, like you, I really hope, my roses

D◉ DOC SPOT 1 Hampton Court

1 Comprehension

Present the text and comprehension questions as standard. When the students understand the topic, play the Doc Spot.

The answers are:

A King Henry VIII
B George III
C Queen Victoria
D George II

2 Listen for detail

2 Writing

This easy task focuses on points of interest in the Doc Spot.

Use the language in the exercise to check for any difficulties in handling comparatives and superlatives. Comparison will be dealt with in detail in Unit 10, but incidental practice such as this should be used to ensure that the basic methods of comparison are understood.

Possible answers are:

A more than any
B much smaller than it is
C one of the finest
D the most well known
E wiser

3 Drill

3 Letter

Encourage the students to use their imagination. They may want to complain about different aspects of being lost in the maze:

    no nighttime patrols   litter in the maze
    untidy bushes   inefficient staff
or even
    monsters, devils and other strangers in the maze

4 What is the secret of the maze?

Let the students quickly solve the 'Conundrum' maze in Unit 1.

Check whether any students know the secret of mazes. Then let the students solve the Hampton Court maze and consider the hint.

Not all the students will want to know the answer – it can take the pleasure away from visiting mazes! The solution lies in the fact that in traditional mazes, unbroken contact with either the left or the right-hand wall will eventually lead to the centre. It does at Hampton Court. However, although sure, this method is slow, as many blind alleys must be explored.

5 Tourist attractions and you

Divide the class into small groups (3 or 4) and ask each group to write out a large advertisement for their favourite tourist attraction. For example, a river trip, a visit to a market, a palace, a temple, a waterfall. Each group should make and hang up a poster, and present the tourist attraction to the rest of the class, trying to persuade them to visit their attraction. At the end of the activity, students can vote on which place they would most like to visit. The group who attracts the highest number of visitors is the winner. This type of activity can be useful in allowing quiet students a chance to speak in front of others without being criticised for mistakes.

D⬛ DOC SPOT 2   Making it big

1   Comprehension

Present the text as standard, and then play the Doc Spot. Use the matching exercise as part of the vocabulary explanation.

The answers are:

A 2)   **B** 1)   **C** 4)   **D** 5)   **E** 3)   **F** 6)

2   Writing

This activity can be extended to include the students' reactions to whatever song is the most popular locally during the week of the lesson.

3   Interview

Illustrations from pop magazines can be used to provide information about clothes, life-style, etc. It may be possible to show the class video recordings of well-known pop groups for discussion. These could be used as a basis for the students' preparation, and then as an introduction to the interviews.

4   Puzzle

The students can copy the puzzle out if necessary. This type of puzzle is very easy to construct. As a group competition, get the students to make up puzzles for the rest of the class to solve.

The answers are:

A Bowie	**D** Jagger	**G** Ferry
B Wonder	**E** Lennon	**H** Sting
C Dylan	**F** Jackson	**I** Presley

Boy George is the name that appears in the puzzle if all the answers are correct.

This topic can be extended into a general discussion about pop music. Do the students like it? Who are their favourite artists? Students could bring in their own audio- or videocassettes for discussion in class.

 CONUNDRUM

1   Destinations

Time is an important part of a suspect's alibi – and so are the suspect's whereabouts. This viewing guide helps the students understand who is doing what at the time of the murder and shortly after.

The answers are:

Maurice Hutchinson	destination unknown
Felicity Curran	travelling to Munich
Alec Lee	staying at the hotel

2   The victim's identity

The students should appreciate the significance of the lack of fingerprints: someone has wiped the gun clean – unless Kelly is lying.

The correct order is:

D, F, B, A, C, E

3   Whodunnit?

This word is used colloquially to refer to any novel, play or film about murder mysteries: *It's a whodunnit.* Agatha Christie wrote very many whodunnits, and the students may have read her work in translation.

LANGUAGE STUDY

1   What will happen in the future?
and
2   What are you going to do?

Be sure that the students understand that 'going to' is used in English to express a personal intention or plan. Using *will* incorrectly can lend their speech an unnatural sound.

If the class copes satisfactorily with the content of the Language Study, then introduce the following two exceptions. The 'will' form is used in immediate response to a sudden event, for example:

- At home, the door bell rings. One member of the family is about to move towards the door to answer it and says *I'll go!*
- A group of people are walking along, and one loses a piece of paper which the wind carries away. One person shouts *I'll get it!* and runs after it.

This is expressing an immediate intention and taking decisive action; in effect, it tells other people that the situation is under control.

Similarly, *will* can be used with emphasis to show that the speaker is determined to do something. For example, early in the day a workman says *I hope to finish it by this evening* or *I'm going to finish it this evening.* Later, after a very difficult day this could become *I will finish it this evening, don't worry!*

These exceptions are dealt with further in Unit 3.

Exercise 1

Most British tabloid newspapers and magazines include a daily, weekly or monthly horoscope. If these are available, you can supplement this exercise with predictions for the day or week you are taking the class.

Exercise 2

Sample answers are:

The plane will arrive at Heathrow airport at 8pm.
I'm going shopping tomorrow afternoon.
I'm going to the cinema with Bill on Tuesday.
It's going to rain.
The race will start at 2.30pm.
I'm going out to dinner tonight with a friend.
I'm going for a walk in the park.

3 Is Billy's future certain or uncertain?

4 Drill

Exercise 3

certain to happen:	He will miss his coffee.
likely to happen:	He'll probably have to work through lunch.
	He's just about ready to resign.
unlikely to happen:	He'd rather be a detective.

NB: 'I'm just about to . . .' or 'I'm ready to . . .' mean that something is likely to happen.
'I'm just about ready to . . .' is a little less likely.

4 Hope and expectation

Exercise 4

Also encourage students to use the affirmative:
You should get there on time.
I hope we'll get there on time.

KEY WORDS AND PHRASES

5 Pronunciation

UNIT 3

What will you have?

Expressing intentions and making offers

The main aim of this unit is to develop the students' ability to talk about aspects of the future, and to use the 'will' future to express intentions and to make offers. This unit is linked thematically with Unit 2.

PRE-VIEWING PREPARATION

SIT COM:
1 Exaggeration
2 A clairvoyant
3 Who's who?

DOC SPOTS:
Babies reading passage and **1 Comprehension**

London Transport reading passage and **1 Comprehension**

CONUNDRUM:
1 The neighbour
2 The victim's wife

LANGUAGE REVIEW

In this unit you have extended the ways in which you can talk about the future, and have practised

1 expressing immediate intentions and making offers:
I'll have an orange juice.
I'll answer it!

2 making predictions with 'if' and 'when':
If I'm caught, I'll be put in prison.
When a child gets bored, he'll shout for his mother.

3 talking about past intentions:
I was going to visit my sister, but I stayed at home.

4 talking about future activities:
By this time tomorrow, I'll be sitting at home.

5 expressing present and past expectations:
I'm glad it's Saturday tomorrow.
I'm looking forward to tomorrow.
He wasn't looking forward to it.

KEY WORDS AND PHRASES

according to
against the law
to ban
to be banned
behaviour
a breakdown
a circumstance
a circus
a clairvoyant
clever
a company
a composer
a computer
a crystal ball
a debt

DECISIONS
You can take decisions, make a decision, or come to a decision. Decide which one you like!

delicate
despite
difficult
to disturb
a drain
an electrician
elegant
an emphasis
an estimate
eventually
a fare
to gamble
honestly

to identify
in effect
instead
an instrument
to intend
to kid someone (*colloquial*)
life expectancy
lots and lots
lots of things
a maternity ward
to mention
mineral water
a musician
nowadays
a parking ticket
a pianist
population
to predict
to push around

CHICKEN MARENGO
A chicken casserole. Chicken cooked in white wine and seasoned with pepper, mushrooms and tomatoes.
This dish was allegedly cooked for the Emperor Napoleon of France at the Battle of Marengo, in Italy, against the Austrians in 1800.

MONEY MATTERS
We're spending too much.
We're throwing money down the drain.
It costs a fortune.
It's more trouble than it's worth.
The fares were cut.

a reaction
ready
to repair
a representative
to respond
second-best
a shopping list
to shout
to specialise in
to spend
terrible
a town house
useful
urgent
a violinist
to visit
a weather forecast

PHRASES
Don't mention it.
It strikes me as a . . .
She's meant to . . .
Fancy meeting you here!
You don't mind if I . . .
Would you mind if I . . .
As a matter of fact, . . .
In the course of his work . . .
He had something on his mind.

 SIT COM

1 Exaggeration

This task contains quotes from the video. Be sure that the students understand the sentences before playing the sequence.

It is important that students appreciate that this type of exaggeration is common in British English; nobody takes the remarks seriously, and nobody is offended by the jokes.

The viewing guide can be used as cues for the students to call out when they identify the speakers. At this stage in the unit, the students are not concerned with the language features which form the expressions used; they should concentrate on the element of exaggeration. Return to this guide at a later stage, when Language Study 2 **What will happen if . . . ?** is dealt with.

The answers are:

Mrs Belmont	×
Billy	×
Billy	×
Sarah	×
Mr Stenhouse	√
Mr Stenhouse	√

2 A clairvoyant

This task is very similar to **1 Exaggeration.** It contains many quotes from the video and should be thoroughly prepared with the students in advance. Students can also discuss further uses for a computer.

Check answers against the video and/or the video script.

3 Who's who?

The answers are:

A Billy, an office boy
B Sherlock Holmes, a detective
C Gustav Mahler, a composer

Gustav Mahler (1860–1911), was an Austrian conductor and prolific composer of symphonies and song cycles.

Sherlock Holmes is one of the most famous detectives in the world, but is entirely fictional. He was created by Sir Arthur Conan Doyle (1859–1930), a Scottish doctor who gave up medicine to be a writer. Holmes' address at 221B Baker Street, London, has never existed; but letters to him are answered by the commercial company that occupies the site where the house would have been.

The most famous quotation from Sherlock Holmes, *'Elementary, my dear Watson',* is also fictitious. It is supposedly based on the following quote from *The Crooked Man:*

> *'Excellent!' I cried.*
> *'Elementary,' said he.*

4 The parking meter

The answer is: £10

Offences against the law for things such as speeding and parking wrongly are not counted as criminal offences in English law. A traffic offence is part of civil law. Ask the class to discover whether there are such differences in their country.

D◉ DOC SPOT 1 Babies

1 Comprehension

Present the text and the comprehension questions as standard. When the students understand the topic, play the Doc Spot.

Note that a quote from this printed text will be used later in Language Study **2 What will happen if . . .?**

The answers are:

A No. It is (only) estimated that the population will be six thousand million by the year 2000.

B Babies born nowadays can expect to live longer than those born twenty years ago.

C The population increase in Britain is not very high because families are smaller than they used to be.

D Dr Jolly is a paediatrician – a doctor who specialises in children's health and behaviour.

E A child can get bored quickly if he is left playing on his own, without his mother watching.

F The child should drop the bad behaviour because it doesn't get any encouragement.

1 Listen for detail

2 Writing

This transfer exercise may need preparation with some classes. The exercise can be used for homework or private study.

Sample answers are:

A Six thousand million people is the estimated world population in the year 2000.

B Babies born twenty years ago have a shorter life expectancy than those born nowadays.

C Local hospitals run classes for mothers-to-be.

D Children's health and behaviour is the special concern of Dr Jolly.

E I will come, but only if you shout at me.

F Helping parents understand what goes on in a child's mind is the (main) emphasis of child care today.

3 Dictionary work

This gives students the opportunity to practise their scanning skills. Use the words in the exercise as a quick quiz before the students use their dictionaries. Students may recognise some of the terms from their own experience or international medical usage.

The answers are:

A specialises in treating minor ailments of the feet

B specialises in treating the female reproductive system

C specialises in treating and correcting deformities in bones or muscles

D specialises in treating skin diseases

E specialises in treating hair and its diseases

F specialises in treating children

G specialises in the study of nutrition and diet

H specialises in treating eye diseases

I specialises in the study of ageing and treating old people's problems

J specialises in treating the nervous system

 2 Pronunciation

4 Puzzle

The figures in brackets indicate how many letters are in each word.

The answers are:

A late	**E** Dover	**I** approve
B real	**F** value	**J** prelate (a difficult one!)
C leave	**G** repeat	
D plate	**H** propel	

5 Children and you

This exercise gives further practice of *should* and *shouldn't*, introduced in Unit 2.

Views about the relationship between parents and children are often governed by cultural or economic factors. Let the students discuss the matter freely.

D⦿ DOC SPOT 2   London Transport

1 Comprehension

Present the text as standard, then play the Doc Spot through once. Prepare the true/false questions with the class. Play the Doc Spot through again, with pauses after each piece of information for the students to take notes. Check the answers. If necessary play the Doc Spot again – either for enjoyment, or to show the students where their errors are.

The answers are:

A ×   **B** ×   **C** ×   **D** ×   **E** √

 3 Listen for meaning

2 Opposites

This can be treated as a written or oral exercise.

The answers are:

A The tube is the slowest way of getting about London.

B Tube fares used to be cheap.

C Far fewer people are using the tube than ever before.

D Few passengers are happy with the service.

E He can see a reason why buskers should be banned. (or 'some reasons')

F Most people would rather not hear music.

3 Problem solving

This activity is linked loosely to the opening scene of the Sit Com in Unit 2.

The problem solving can be adapted in two ways.
- students make up their own problems from the London Underground map
- students adapt the exercise to maps of public transport in their own areas: they must imagine that they have to explain the journey to a foreign visitor

In the central area of London, journeys by underground take on average 2 minutes per station, including waiting for the train, entering and leaving the station, and changing. On the Victoria Line, the trains are fully automatic, and do not need drivers. However, there is one in the cab, just to reassure passengers. Buskers are a common sight in the London Underground.

Check answers against the map.

 4 Pronunciation

4 Public transport and you

The standard of public transport, and the economics of it, vary widely around the world. Generally speaking, there is less state subsidy in Britain for public transport than there is in many other Western European countries. The students may wish to discuss this issue, or they can express their opinions in a written exercise for homework.

CONUNDRUM

1 The neighbour

This guide provides the students with new vocabulary so they can describe this new character. Prepare the vocabulary, then play the first part of 'Conundrum'. Stop the video, check and discuss the students' opinions. If necessary, play the section again. Do not play on until the next task has been prepared.

2 The victim's wife

This guide allows the students to talk about and interpret what they see. Go through the list of activities, checking that the students understand what they are; use mime if necessary.

Before playing the scene for the first time, turn down the sound control on the television set and play the scene with vision only. This will allow students to concentrate on watching what Mrs Gibbs does. Check that they agree on her actions. Rewind the video, turn the sound control up and play the scene again, letting the students concentrate on the dialogue. Then show the scene a third time and ask the students to interpret the widow's actions.

The answers are: **B, E**

3 The victim

The main aim of these guides is to focus attention on the Gibbs as a married couple; and the fact that Mr Gibbs legally carried a pistol (that is quite unusual in Britain).

The answers are:

A He never travelled abroad on business. He was sometimes away for a few days in Britain.

B 3) √

4 Discussion

Be sure that the students understand the heavy irony of Mrs Taylor's remark *'that nice Mr Gibbs'*.

LANGUAGE STUDY

1 What will you have?

The short *'ll* form used here should be practised by the students in role plays set in restaurants or bars.

Exercise 1

Elicit the answers to this exercise from the class. Make a general request, and encourage the students to respond as quickly as possible. For example:

> **You:** Can we have a window open, please?
> **Student:** I'll open it!

Sample answers are:

A I'll get it!/answer it!   E I'll pay!
B I'll catch it!/get it!   F I'll (run and) get it!
C I'll go!   G I'll (climb up and) get it!
D I'll save her!   H I'll catch him!

5 Drill and 6 Drill

2 What will happen if . . .?

Exercise 2

The simple conditionals *If . . ., I'll . . .* should not be a problem for students. Depending on the level of the class, introduce the often problematic *unless* in preparation for more detailed study in Unit 6 Language Study.

Unless can be used with both positive and negative sentences.
a) I won't go unless you pay. = If you don't pay, I won't go.
b) I'll go unless you don't pay. = If you pay, I'll go.
c) I won't go unless you don't pay. = If you pay, I won't go.
d) I'll go unless you pay. = If you don't pay, I'll go.
a) and b) have the same meaning; c) and d) have the same meaning.
c) is the most unlikely sentence, although it could be used in certain circumstances.

You can extend Exercises 1 and 2 by asking the students to convert their sentences to *unless* constructions, if possible. Or return to these after the students have completed Unit 6.

3 I was going away, but . . .

Exercise 3

Make sure that the students notice the stress patterns in this use of the past continuous. In the narrative sense, *was* is unstressed [wəz]; in the past intentional use, *was* is usually stressed [woz]:

[wəz] I was 'going to 'visit my 'sister, when . . .
[woz] I 'was going to 'visit my 'sister, but . . .

Exercise 4

The use of the continuous form after *'will be sitting'* emphasises the duration of the action.

Exercise 5

The answers are:

Mrs Belmont . . .

. . . was looking forward to Saturday.

. . . was looking forward to watching the Western on television.

. . . was looking forward to spending the weekend with her sister.

. . . was not looking forward to the journey.

Invite the students to give as many reasons as they can to support what they say about what they are personally looking forward to. If they need prompting, use questions like:

What are you looking forward to in particular?

Why are you looking forward to that?

Why aren't you looking forward to that?

KEY WORDS AND PHRASES

When presenting 'MONEY MATTERS', point out to the students the difference between *priceless* (ie extremely expensive, no price can be put on it), and *worthless* or *valueless* (ie very cheap, having no value).

---

 7   Pronunciation and intonation   (This also relates to Exercise 3.)

UNIT 4

What have you been doing?

Talking about the past (1)

The main aim of this unit is to extend the students' ability to talk about events in the past and present. In particular, the distinction between narration and description is made clear. Narration requires a sequence of events, and uses the past simple, the past continuous and the past perfect tenses.

Description need not have a sequence, and in this unit is exemplified by the present perfect, the present perfect continuous, and 'used to'.

The theme of past time is continued in Unit 5.

PRE-VIEWING PREPARATION

SIT COM:	1 At the travel agent's
	3 Travellers
	5 Billy, master detective
	6 Ted's car is back

DOC SPOTS: **Charles Dickens** reading passage and **1 Comprehension**

Isambard Kingdom Brunel reading passage and **1 Comprehension** (optional)

CONUNDRUM: **1 Alec Lee's alibi**

LANGUAGE REVIEW

In this unit you have practised

1 talking about repeated activities that have been going on for some time using the present perfect continuous:
I've been getting these stomach pains.

2 talking about habits and descriptions of what you used to do and no longer do using *used to:*
I used to have the same problem, but not now.

3 telling a story using the past continuous and the past simple:
I was going into the office when I noticed a man near the car.

4 placing an event in a narrative using the past perfect:
Brunel designed the bridge over the Avon; he had won a competition.

5 describing what has happened in a situation using the present perfect:
Where's my money? You haven't paid me!

KEY WORDS AND PHRASES

abroad
an achievement
an alibi
an audience
bad-tempered
boring
to bring to justice
to capture
a car chase
a car thief
to clasp
a competition
curious
dangerous
a design
eager
a fault
a genius
hips

HOLIDAYS

British people love the seaside. There are many seaside resorts along the coast, with sandy beaches – but not enough sun. 'At the seaside' suggests children and beach activities; 'on the coast' is more neutral, or used for adults only.

justice
a medal
a network
notorious
a novelist
to peer
phenomenal
a pilot
a pioneer
popularity

to realise
to reflect
to be reflected
a reminder
to resign
to be resigned to
to restore
rich food
a row
ruthless

AMERICAN ENGLISH

laid back (*American*) = relaxed (*British*)
neat (*British*) = tidy, well-groomed
neat (*American*) = great, very good

ACHES & PAINS

stomachache
stomach pains
back ache
earache
headache
nerves
I'm not feeling well.

single-handed
a snob
a steward
to struggle
transatlantic
a travel agent's
to treat badly
unthinkable
a villain

COLLOQUIALISMS

to nip to pinch, to squeeze between two points, (or) to go quickly
a pal a friend
Oi! is used to attract attention without being polite.
Eh? suggests a query or question.
Oh gosh! is a polite way of expressing surprise.

▷ SIT COM

1 At the travel agent's

This opening scene has no dialogue. The viewing guide provides the students with adjectives which they can use to describe what they see.

Illustrate the three actions of the lady in the travel agent's by miming. Check that the students understand, then play the sequence. Encourage the students to mime the adjectives listed.

The answers to the second part are:
A 1)   **B** 3)   **C** 2)

2 Car thief

This exercise in narration is used later in the Language Study section. Note that here the full form of the past continuous verb is used:

> . . . (a man) was struggling with the car door.

Compare this with the ellipsis of the policewoman's question to Billy, when he is later questioned:

> And what did you do when you saw this man stealing the car?

This is preferable to

> And what did you do when you saw this man *who was* stealing the car?

The second version has an adjectival, classification effect – as though there were other men who were doing different things whom Billy also saw. Classifying clauses are the subject of **3 Transfer exercise** in Doc Spot 1.

Check answers against the video or against the video script.

3 Travellers

The places listed in the viewing guide should help students follow this dialogue about travelling. Prepare the place names before viewing the sequence.

The answers are:
Billy has been nowhere.
Sarah has been to North Africa, Tenerife and the Middle East.
Joe has been to Italy.

1   Listen for detail

4 Billy, the witness

This task will make the students aware of how difficult it is to accurately describe somebody. After the students have completed the guide, and listened to Billy's bad description, split them into groups of 2 or 3. Remind them that they also saw the car thief, and ask them to write out a description of him for the police.

Check the description of each group for language accuracy, then replay the scene to see which group's description is the most accurate.

5 Billy, master detective

Prepare the vocabulary items in this text before playing the scene; this will help students follow the fantasy sequence. The writing task can be used for homework or private study.

Check answers against the video and/or the video script.

6   Ted's car is back

The humorous ending to the episode will be clear to the students. This guide gives the students some more vocabulary to talk about what they see. Prepare the vocabulary with the students before viewing the sequence.

D◉ DOC SPOT 1   Charles Dickens

1   Comprehension

Present the text and comprehension questions as standard. When the students understand the topic, play the Doc Spot.

Sample answers are:

A No, he was a novelist. (However, he did write some poems.)
B His work was published in monthly parts which were sold quite cheaply.
C Yes, partly because he was a genius whose work is still relevant to this century.
D He lived there for two years.
E No, it's now a museum.
F The death of his sister-in-law, Mary Hogarth.

 2   Listen for detail

2   Completion dialogue

Explain to the students that the answers required here are not just quotes from the text. In speech, a more colloquial, relaxed style should be used.

Sample dialogue:

Tourist:	Excuse me. Can you help me?
You:	Yes, of course.
Tourist:	Does Charles Dickens still live here?
You:	No. He's dead.
Tourist:	Oh. When did he die?
You:	Over one hundred years ago – in 1870.
Tourist:	How stupid of me! Did he live here all this life?
You:	No, just for two years.
Tourist:	I see. And did he write any of his famous books here?
You:	Yes, he did. He completed *The Pickwick Papers* while he was living here and he wrote *Nicholas Nickleby* and *Oliver Twist*.
Tourist:	Thank you for your help.
You:	My pleasure.

3   Transfer exercise

This transfer exercise focuses on the classifying nature of subordinate clauses. The example contains

> . . . a house which is now a museum

suggesting that there may be other houses which are not museums. This is similar to the language point outlined in the notes to **2 Car thief** in the Sit Com.

The answers are:

A I used to know a boy who is now an MP.
B Harry studied at a school which is now a prison.
C Tessa wrote a song which is now in the Top Twenty.
D I worked with a girl who is now a beauty queen.

4 Mixed up names

This exercise gives students a further opportunity to do some research using reference books.

The answers are:

A Oliver Twist
B Nicholas Nickleby
C Pickwick Papers
D Bleak House
E Little Dorrit

F A Christmas Carol
G The Old Curiosity Shop
H David Copperfield
I Great Expectations
J Martin Chuzzlewit

3 Pronunciation

5 Writers and you

This task is also suitable for written work or it can be extended. Groups can undertake research into various aspects of a famous writer's life and works, and prepare a portrait of the writer following the style of the Doc Spot video on Dickens.

D◉ DOC SPOT 2   Isambard Kingdom Brunel

Present the text as standard. When the topic is understood, play the Doc Spot.

1 Comprehension

The matching exercise can be used at any stage:
- as a private study and research introduction to the topic, before the summary is read
- as immediate follow up
- as homework or private study after viewing

The answers are:

A 3)   B 5)   C 1)   D 2)   E 4)   F 6)

2 Spot the mistakes

This exercise develops intensive reading skills. The activity can be extended by providing groups of students with texts on any topic that suits them. Each group uses the text given to them as the basis for composing a similar text which contains errors. They then give their new text, with the original, for solution. Groups can work in competition with other groups, but in cooperation within the groups. A game can also be played to identify which text is correct and which is false.

Check the answers against the reading passage.

3 Pioneers

This activity is a further extension of information retrieval practice.

Students can also research locally well-known pioneers, inventors or discoverers.

A Italian navigator who discovered the Bahamas, Cuba, the West Indies, and the lowlands of South America
B Portuguese navigator who discovered a sea route to India via the Cape of Good Hope
C English scientist who discovered the theory of gravitation
D Scottish-born American, inventor of the telephone
E Italian pioneer of radio waves as a means of communication

F German-born American who discovered the theory of relativity
G Scottish pioneer of television
H English inventor of the jet engine

4 Inventions and you

If the students move into the absurd, then they will be following a well trodden path for English eccentrics. Machines to feed the pet dog, to wake people up, or to catch household mice, are a favourite theme for doodlers. The most famous inventor of ridiculous machines is Heath Robinson, whose name has become part of the language to mean something ridiculously complicated and unworkable – 'a Heath Robinson solution'.

If suitable, ask students to draw their own inventions. Other students must then guess what the inventions are supposed to do.

 CONUNDRUM

1 Alec Lee's alibi

The students must appreciate the need for all the main characters to have an alibi. This guide is used again in Language Study Exercise 4.

The answers are:
A 5) B 6) C 2) D 1) E 3) F 4)

2 Kelly's information

This establishes that Kelly had met the murdered man before.

The answers are:
A, D, E, F

3 Discussion

The students' motivation to speculate and to formulate ideas – and yet be wrong – must be maintained throughout the 15 episodes. This discussion allows them to check with their own first impressions.

LANGUAGE STUDY

1 What have you been doing?

The main aim of this section is to make it clear to students that the present perfect continuous form relates to the present and is not rooted in the past. This is shown in two ways. Firstly, the examples given relate the construction closely to present tense descriptions of what people are like, what they do, and what happens to them – or what is happening all the time. Secondly, the quoted examples of the fat person and the person who has been dieting deliberately place the continuous form in different parts of the short texts. This is to emphasise that in these short descriptive pieces, the sequence of the facts does not matter: the fat person could have said:

I've been eating too much for years –
I'm fat. In fact, I'm always eating.
I eat too much.

This flexibility in the order is in complete contrast to the fixed sequence that is required in narration.

Exercise 1

The exercise can be prepared orally, using both positive and negative sentences as answers. The students can then write out the answers for homework or private study.

The answers are:
A 5)   **B** 1)   **C** 6)   **D** 2)   **E** 3)   **F** 4)

 4   Drill

2   I used to, but I don't now

This should be fairly straightforward revision of the *used to* construction. The negative sentences are slightly more difficult to use and say fluently.

The negative form *used not to* is now less common than *didn't used to* and is rarely used in speech.

Exercise 2

Free answers.

 5   Now repeat these sentences   and   6   Drill

3   Story telling: I was going into the office when . . .

The students must appreciate the difference in communicative function between the past simple tense and the past continuous tense. If we have, for example, three past simple tense forms, then we also have a short story:

> Ted *shouted* at Billy, who *walked* angrily out of the office, and *went* down the street.

A similar list of past continuous forms sets the scene, but does not advance the narrative:

> The FOLLOW THROUGH staff *were arguing* furiously; Billy *was getting* angrier and angrier. Ted's face *was going* purple with anger, when . . .

After the *when*, we expect the narrative.

If we have instead:

> They argued furiously; Billy got angry and Ted's face went purple with anger . . .

then we have changed the communicative function. This account of their emotions is now part of a sequential narrative.

English language authors can of course use this feature for stylistic effects. As an extension activity, provide the class with texts containing both types of construction. Let them analyse the texts, listing in one column all the past simple examples, in another all the past continuous forms. The first list, when read out, will tell a story. The second list will not.

Exercise 3

Check answers against Sit Com **2 Car thief**.

4   Story telling: He had won a competition . . .

If there are no other language features present, apart from the *had* construction, then the past perfect just locates an action earlier in the given narrative (as in the example in this section). For reasons of style, many English writers use clauses such as *After he had . . .* , *When he had . . .* even through the displacement of time is indicated by the construction on its own.

Exercise 4

Sample answer:

Lee's plane was scheduled to arrive at 17.00, but it had arrived at 16.58. He registered at the hotel at 18.00 after he had exchanged a few words with Matthew Gibbs. Just before 8 o'clock he had coffee with Bernie Raistrick with whom he had had dinner.

5   You haven't paid me!

The main aim of this exercise is to strengthen the link between the present simple and the present perfect. The students should note that the taxi driver makes no reference to time: his comments spring from the situation as he is describing it. The alternatives given for what he could say show that the present tense forms are used to describe a situation.

This theme is taken up in Unit 5 Language Study.

Exercise 5

The answers are:
A You've forgotten your umbrella.
B You haven't shut the door.
C You haven't given me a cup of tea.
D I've bought a new coat.
E Why has he gone to Scotland?

UNIT 5

Tell us about the stars you've met!

Talking about the past (2)

AIMS

The main aim of this unit is to develop further the students' ability to talk about past and present events. It follows on from Unit 4.

Some past tense forms, such as the present perfect, are presented to the students in a present context, allied to some aspects of description. The language of advertisements is used to make the relationship between the tense forms clear.

PRE-VIEWING PREPARATION

SIT COM:
1 **At the watchmaker's shop**
2 **Julie's mother**
3 **How do they feel?**

DOC SPOTS:
Bristol City Football Club reading passage and
1 Comprehension (optional)

Whitstable oysters reading passage and **1 Comprehension** (optional)

CONUNDRUM:
1 **Kelly, the hotel waiter**
2 **Maxwell and the manager**

LANGUAGE REVIEW

In this unit you have extended your range of ways of talking about events in the past and present. You have practised

1 describing what people have done:
Tell us about the programmes you've made.

2 writing the language of advertisements:
It is wonderful. It has sold millions. Buy one – you will enjoy it!

3 reporting speech from the present tense:
I haven't → I said that I didn't have

4 reporting speech from the past tense:
I meant it → I said that I had meant it

5 and you have also looked at some of the features of hesitant or polite language, using 'if' clauses with 'would' and the past continuous, and using extra adverbs such as 'really':
I was wondering if you'd . . .
I'd really like to . . .

48

approximately
an aristocrat
to arrange
baseball
basketball
behaviour
boastful
bric-a-brac
a cap
to collect
a contract
a curio
digital
to dismiss
embarrassed
to employ
an experience
an explanation
a flashback
flight control
to flourish
a freezer
full-time
to give up

a grandfather clock
a grand piano
hardly
hesitant
intense
to knock
a lie
a manager
to mend
a motive
nostalgic
once
an oyster
professional
a quality player
rude
to sack (*colloquial*)
a secret
secretly
self-assured
to shoot a film
skilful
a spectator
a standard lamp

strict
suspicious
a tapestry
to tell lies
a ticket

TIME
last Tuesday
the other day
for three weeks
in three days
once or twice
three years ago
When were you last there?
yet
temporarily
recently
never
rather a lot
lately
just, just now
Note **just** = only, merely
   just = correct, proper

to be trapped
to trap
to upset someone
a Vice-Chairman
vulgar
a witness

PHRASES
I was minding my own business.
It wasn't a very big lie.
It was the best thing he'd ever done.
The boss was always shouting.
That's almost as good.
I said he didn't know what he was missing.

GUIDE TO THE UNIT

 SIT COM

1   At the watchmaker's shop

This viewing guide allows the students to interpret what they see, and provides them with the vocabulary they need to talk about the sequence.

Run through the viewing guide, checking comprehension, play the sequence, then complete the task.

The answers are:
Billy is: **B** √   **C** √
Julie thinks: **B** √

2   Julie's mother

The living room is crowded with many objects, some of which are referred to by Julie's mother. The checklist in the guide can be used as the basis for a quiz:
   – check the list for comprehension
   – play the sequence, using the pause button to freeze the picture
   – give the class 90 seconds to identify as many of the objects as possible (or have competing groups)

The following are *not* in the living room:
a grand piano, a grandfather clock, a portrait of Julie's father

3 How do they feel?

Note that the reactions of the characters change as the scene progresses.
Billy could be described as boastful, hesitant and nervous.
Julie could be described as insistent, ironic and suspicious.
Julie's mother could be described as enthusiastic, helpful, naive and nostalgic.

4 Where have you been?

This exercise can be left until Language Study **1 Tell us about the stars you've met** has been worked through with the class. It can be prepared by students for homework and then discussed in class.

1 Drill

5 Bric-a-brac

Bric-a-brac and curios are often bought in second-hand shops or at jumble sales. People donate items to jumble sales free of charge: something that keeps reappearing (because nobody wants to keep it at home) is called a 'white elephant'. The profits from jumble sales usually go to charities and good causes.

Valuable articles which are very old are bought and sold by antique dealers.

D◉ DOC SPOT 1   Bristol City Football Club

Present the text as standard. When the class understand the topic, play the Doc Spot.

1 Comprehension

The 'spot the mistakes' questions can be dealt with before or after viewing, either in class or for homework.

Check answers against reading passage.

2 Reported speech

This activity can be left until Language Study **2 Reported speech** has been worked through with the class.

The answers are:
A Terry said that they couldn't buy quality players.
B Terry said that they'd got to get people that cost nothing.
C Terry said that all their players were free transfers.
D Terry said that he could see some of those lads playing in the First Division.
E Leslie Kew said that the club had had success and had then quickly come to failure.
F Leslie Kew said that they had been paying high wages.

3 Spot the mistakes

This is an easy exercise in scanning. If the class is interested, draw comparisons between the British way of recording football results, and the local way.

The mistakes are:
1) Luton had no goals so Walsh couldn't have scored.
2) Total score for Coventry should be 3.
3) Wrong half-time score for Everton.

4) Liverpool's total score incorrect – players shown to have scored 6 goals.

5) Name of scorer for Hamburg is not given.

6) Hamburg is not an English First Division team.

4 Spot the ball

This type of competition is widespread in regional British newspapers. The winning entry must mark the centre of the cross [×] in the centre of the missing football.

The prize money for this type of quiz is relatively small: probably less than an average week's wages.

5 Puzzle

The answers are:

A football	**D** talented	**G** division
B defender	**E** contract	**H** chairman
C transfer	**F** problems	

6 Football and you

The project activities can be developed into a full-scale analysis of UK soccer, if the class is interested. For example, students can prepare league tables, profiles of clubs or leading players, or UK teams in international soccer.

D DOC SPOT 2   Whitstable Oysters

Present the text as standard. When the class understand the topic, play the Doc Spot.

1 Comprehension

The matching definition exercise can be used as preparatory dictionary work, as homework or private study.

The answers are:

A 3)   **B** 2)   **C** 4)   **D** 5)   **E** 6)   **F** 1)

---

2 Listen for detail

---

2 An interview with Ogie

The results of this exercise can be used as additional material for practice in reported speech, if required.

Ogies replies could be:

- It was in about 1925.
- The Violet.
- Yes, we caught oysters and shrimps.
- We got 19 shillings.
- 95 pence. That's less than £1.

3 What's the difference?

This exercise draws together many of the points of language analysis covered in the Language Study sections of this Unit and of Unit 4.

A 1) means Ogie is still living there
    2) implies that Ogie is no longer alive

B 1) refers to a habit or repeated action in the past
    2) means they have grown accustomed to rowing – it refers to present time

C 1) refers to something that they did repeatedly in the past
   2) refers to one event, in the past perfect tense – part of a sequence

D 1) bad weather cannot harm them (because something protects them from it)
   2) bad weather protects them (from something else)

3   Drill

4   Nostalgia and you

What is worth remembering is often culture-bound. Extend the activity by asking the students if there are things that they know about (eg 17th century farm buildings) which in some countries are respected, and in others not.

 CONUNDRUM

The murder was committed in the hotel, and clearly there is something strange about the manager, or Kelly or both.

1   Kelly, the hotel waiter

This guide establishes Kelly and his activities for the students; he is referred to later in the story.

The answers are:

A √   **B** ×   **C** √   **D** ×   **E** √   **F** ×

The answer to **B** may provoke discussion.

2   Maxwell and the manager

The manager allows himself a wry joke:

  Maxwell: Sacked him? That seems rather sudden.
  Manager: There didn't seem to be any way of doing it gradually.

The answers are open to interpretation.

3   The manager

Collect the students' views on the manager for comparison in a later episode.

4   Flashback

The method of analysis for solving this problem of register is outlined for the students in Language Study **3 Register.** The most informal solution is often the one with the shortest sentence. However, the most formal solution is not always the longest sentence. Gibbs' use of *'do'* in **C** makes the invitation more formal than the one in **B**.

A suitable conversation would be: **A, C, A, B, C**

Notice how no reply is made to the questions 'Everything okay?' and 'And how are you?'. This is not uncommon in relatively informal conversation.

5   Flashback again

This exercise can also be used as an extension for **2 Reported speech** in the Language Study section.

Too informal would be: **C, B, B, A, B**
Too formal would be: **B, A, C, C, A**

LANGUAGE STUDY

1 Tell us about the stars you've met!

Many conversations in English start with the present perfect, and then move to the narrative mode. For example, talking about holidays, there might be a few exchanges such as:

> Have you been to . . . ?
> Yes, we've been there several times.

Once an area of common interest is established, then the conversation switches to a narrative account of past experiences:

> We went there a few years ago. We had a . . .

Exercise 1

Free answers. This exercise can be used in class or prepared in class and then completed or extended for homework.

4 Drill

Exercise 2

| COMPLETED TIME: | just now, a moment ago, last Tuesday, in 1984, just |
| UNFINISHED TIME: | ever, never, yet, still, already, since 1975, for the last few minutes, until now |

Exercise 3

The advertisement for gas cookers in Exercise 3 contains language which is a typical style of descriptive prose. If English language magazines are available, then let the class analyse the language structure of the advertisements. The most common features are:

- ★ extended noun phrases, without a verb
- ★ present simple, often with a modal eg *can, must*
- ★ present perfect
- ★ *'will'* future
- ★ imperative forms: Buy one now!

The correct order is: **C, F, G, D, A, E, B**

Exercise 4 is suitable for private study or for homework.

Also complete Sit Com **4 Where have you been?**

2 Reported speech

There is extensive material throughout the unit for further practice in reported speech.

Once students have completed Exercise 4, turn back to the Doc Spot on Bristol City Football Club **2 Reported speech** and complete this exercise, then continue with the exercise suggestions made in Doc Spot 2 and 'Conundrum'.

Note the list of words in Unit 12, Sit Com **2 Politics: the manners,** which can be referred to here. If the verb *to think* is used as an introductory verb, then there is often a switch in the negative particle to outside the reported speech:

> He said, 'I probably won't go.'
> He didn't think that he would go.

However, this is a slightly freer interpretation of reported speech than is usual.

Exercise 5

Possible conversation:

Mrs Belmont: I haven't time to do a full-time job and look after you [a husband] day and night.

Mr Belmont: I'm sorry, dear. I didn't mean to upset you.

3 Register

Other adverbs which typically occur as redundant, with the effect of increasing formality or politeness include *awfully, possibly* and *most*:

> Thanks awfully! (now slightly old-fashioned usage)
>
> Could I possibly close the window?
>
> That really is most kind of you.

Verb constructions similar to the use of *would* include *could* as in the example above, and *might*:

> I wonder if I might ask you to tea?

Few speakers would use the above sentence in modern colloquial English, though it could be used to create effect.

Exercise 6

Possible dialogue:

Billy: Would you like to come out with me?

Julie: Oh! Well, I was thinking of, er, washing my hair tonight. But I suppose I could really do that first. Um, when?

Billy: This evening.

Julie: OK. Well, I could give you my address, if you like.

KEY WORDS AND PHRASES

The use of the past continuous forms in the listed PHRASES emphasises the continuing nature of the activities.

UNIT 6

If you --- I'll ---

Talking about conditions (1)

The main aim of this unit is to consolidate the students' present ability to talk about conditionality. The three main types of conditional sentence are used throughout the unit; these may be known to the students by various names, such as 1st, 2nd and 3rd conditionals; or real and unreal conditions; or conditions which can or cannot be fulfilled.

PRE-VIEWING PREPARATION

SIT COM: **1 Some useful advice**

DOC SPOTS: **Training racehorses** reading passage and **1 Comprehension**
Children talking reading passage and **1 Comprehension**

CONUNDRUM: **1 Any progress?**

LANGUAGE REVIEW

In this unit you have studied conditions and have practised

1 talking about positive conditions:
If you give me the camera, I'll do that for you.

2 talking about negative conditions, using *unless . . .* and *if . . . not . . .*:
Unless you take the lens cap off, it won't work.
If you don't take the lens cap off, you won't get any pictures.

3 talking about wishful thinking, using *If I . . ., I'd . . .*:
If I had a camera, I'd change the whole course of history.

4 talking about things which could come true, using *If you . . ., you'd . . .*:
If you weren't so arrogant, you'd be a nicer person.

5 talking about conditions in the past, using *If you'd . . . I'd have . . .*:
If you'd asked me to do it, I'd have done it.

Note the progression, sometimes called the first conditional, the second conditional, and the third conditional:

1st: If you ask me, I will (I'll) do it.
2nd: If you asked me, I would (I'd) do it.
3rd: If you had (you'd) asked me, I would (I'd) have done it.

6 Introducing conditions using phrases like *in that case, otherwise, just imagine if*, etc.

KEY WORDS AND PHRASES

an article

arrogant

awful

to bring up

to be brought up

a button

CAMERAS

Focus the camera, press the button – and the snap has been taken. Holiday photographs are usually called snaps.
A photo is taken through the lens of the camera; the lens cap protects the lens.

clearly

clockwork

a complaint

confused

COVENT GARDEN

Covent Garden was once a fruit and vegetable market in the heart of London's theatreland. Now it is a centre for quality shops, restaurants – and street theatre.

confusing

to decide on

to disturb

to exchange

extremely

fashionable

to be fed up

fingernails

greenfly

HI-FI

Hi-Fi stands for high fidelity – good quality sound reproduction.
High Tech means high technology – using the latest and most sophisticated technical aids.

healthy

history

a horse

horrible

imminent

in spite of

to intend

to interview

a journalist

a lead

limited

a manager

nevertheless

official

otherwise

PHOTOGRAPHY

How do you say it?
A pho'tographer takes 'photographs – it is a photo'graphic process.

popular

to prepare

to present

to press

to produce

to purchase

a receipt

a reflection

research

a rule

a search warrant

second-hand

to sense

to state

a teenager

to threaten

a tip

a warrant

a wedding

well-known

whereas

PHRASES

I'm very busy.
You don't seem to have very much on.
I can't make up my mind.
He wasn't prepared to help.
There's nothing I can do.

 SIT COM

1 Some useful advice

This simple matching task introduces some conditional forms used in the unit and should be completed before the students view the video.

The answers are:

A 3) **B** 4) **C** 2) **D** 1)

2 At 'Charades'

This viewing task provides the students with vocabulary to talk about the behaviour of the people they see. The modification of the adjective by an adverb is an extension of the use of compound adjectives from earlier units.

Let the students watch the scene once through for general comprehension and visual information. Ask for words to describe the shop assistant and the customer. Check if the students suggest the same words as those in the task. Teach the new words, and play the scene again, concentrating on the task.

Sample answers:

lady: justifiably angry and suitably indignant

the shop assistant: quite unhelpful, coldly correct and formally polite

The 'Charades' shop is full of objects. Use this sequence as the basis for observation games between groups. For example, groups note down things which they see, but add to their lists things which are not in the shop. Other groups have to remember what items on the list are really shown in the sequence. For this activity, the scene can be played with the sound turned down.

3 Greenfly

The answers to the matching exercise are:

A 2) **B** 3) **C** 1) **D** 6) **E** 4) **F** 5)

The second part of this is a fantasy exercise, and the students should be as extreme as they want. Underlying the exercise is the necessity for correct logical steps when describing a process or procedure.

D⦿ DOC SPOT 1   Training racehorses

1 Comprehension

Present the text as standard, and then work through the vocabulary comprehension exercise. When the class understand the topic, play the Doc Spot.

In the UK, track racing of animals is confined to horses (flat races and steeplechases over jumps) and dogs. There is not the tradition of pony trap racing that is found in many countries. Use the documentary as the basis for a discussion about the types of racing that occur locally.

The answers are: **A** 1) **B** 1) **C** 1) **D** 2) **E** 2)

 1 Listen for detail

2 Read and compare

This is an exercise in intensive reading, as details have to be found and corrected. It can be used for private study or homework.

Check the answers against the reading passage.

3 Project

Sport is taken seriously in the UK, and leading national newspapers carry reports and results of matches played between amateur teams and school teams. Use the quiz as the basis for a discussion about local and national sporting occasions.

Here is some further information which the class might like to know (or which they can find out from reference books in their project work):

A The Calcutta Cup is so-called because it was presented to the Rugby Union as a trophy by the East India Company in 1898. Each year, there are matches between the 'home' countries – England, Wales, Scotland, Ireland, and, curiously, France.

B The University Boat Race is held between Oxford and Cambridge. The team colours are blue: Oxford Blue is dark, and Cambridge Blue is light, like cyan.

C The FA Cup Final. The Football Association Cup Final is open to any team in England whereas only professional teams play in the Football League. Scotland has its own cup final.

D Wimbledon. Wimbledon is a suburb in southwest London, on the underground transport system. Membership of the Wimbledon club is very exclusive; it is not only the headquarters of lawn tennis, but also of croquet, an interesting but rather obscure game played on grass with hammer-shaped clubs – croquet is like giant lawn billiards.

E Shoot grouse. Grouse is a game bird, that is, a wild bird with a distinctive flavour, similar to pheasant and partridge. To preserve stocks, the open season for shooting starts on 12th August – known to sportsmen as 'The Glorious Twelfth'.

F December 26th is the day after Christmas Day, and is called Boxing Day. The name has nothing to do with the sport of boxing. It comes from the old habit of giving servants money and gifts in boxes. Nowadays the British give money to their milkman, postman, etc.

4 Puzzle

The first part of the puzzle draws on vocabulary items from the reading passage and from the video.

The answers are:

A horse racing	**D** valuable	**G** Liverpool
B Derby	**E** Grand National	
C trainer	**F** Aintree	

The Grand National is a steeplechase, run every year over a course in Aintree, Liverpool. It is probably as famous as The Derby, attracting millions of bets from people who do not normally bet.

5 Gambling

Cultural attitudes to gambling vary enormously, depending on social, historical, economic and religious pressures. The subject may be suitable for a debate, with speakers for and against the motion that 'Gambling should be banned in all its forms'.

D⬤ DOC SPOT 2   Children talking

1 Comprehension

Present the text and the vocabulary exercise as standard. When the topic is clear to the class, play the Doc Spot.

The answers are:

A 4)   **B** 5)   **C** 2)   **D** 6)   **E** 3)   **F** 1)

2 Listen and repeat

2 Conditionals

The conditionals treated here are typical examples of 'unreal' conditions, or 2nd conditionals.

The use of such conditionals is common in quizzes, in speculation, and in dreams for the future. But all speakers realise that the thing mentioned after *if* probably will not happen. The exercise can be treated now, or in conjunction with the Language Study **3 Wishful thinking!** The students' questions and answers should follow the pattern of the example. Check answers against audio script.

 3 Drill

3 Writing

This allows the students to exercise their imagination further. This activity is picked up in Language Study **3 Wishful thinking!** It is suitable for private study or for homework.

4 Out of the mouths of children

In re-telling their childhood remarks, the students will also be repeating the learning points of Units 4 and 5.

Prompt further responses by asking questions of the story teller and the listeners, such as 'What would you have done if . . .?'.

CONUNDRUM

Phillips and Maxwell make positive progress in this episode by discovering the secret of Gibbs' garage. The secret is not revealed in 'Conundrum' 6, but is made clear at the beginning of 'Conundrum' 7.

1 Any progress?

Prepare the guide with the students before playing this dialogue between Phillips and Maxwell. The guide focuses on potentially difficult language.

The answers are:
A 2) **B** 1) **C** 3) **D** 2) **E** 2) (In some contexts, the answer could be 1).)

2 The Gibbs' house

This guide proves the students with the vocabulary necessary for describing the Gibbs' house – and many others.

The content of the plot in this episode is mainly visual, as the police search the house.
The Gibbs' house has:
a hedge, a garden path, a drive, an integral garage, a lawn with flower beds, fireplaces, radiators and chimney stacks. It is a detached house.

3 The garage

Start speculation among students by asking questions such as:
'What do you think it could be?'
'What do you think the police would do if . . . ?'
'What do you think Mrs Gibbs will say when the police tell her that . . . ?'

LANGUAGE STUDY

1 If you . . . I'll . . .

This recaps on using 1st conditionals to offer help or to give advice which the students have seen in Sit Com **1 Some useful advice** and throughout the unit.

Exercise 1

The answers are:

A If you haven't got any money, I'll lend you some.
B If you carry the little one, I'll carry the big one.

If the students need more practice, this exercise can be extended using vocabulary from **Key words and phrases.**

---

 4 Drill   Offering help

---

2 Unless . . ./If not . . .

Refer back to Unit 3, Language Study 2.

Unless causes many students a problem, even though they can learn that *unless* is the same as *if not*. One of the reasons for the problems lies in the fact that *if not* cannot be followed by a negative verb, whereas *unless not* is good English, even though it is not particularly common.

Exercise 2

Set up pair work exercises as suggested in the Students' Book. Practise with one or more students in front of the whole class first. This exercise should give the students ample scope to practise all forms of *unless* and *if not*. It should also liven up the lesson!

 5 Drill

Notice the use of the word *whereas* in the notes above. Prodip uses *whereas* in the first canteen scene of the Sit Com. He says to Sarah:

I'm rather busy, whereas you don't seem to have very much on at the moment.

(He is, of course, referring to how busy she is, not how much clothing she is wearing.)

The use of *whereas* in conversation is rather formal. He could have said several other words, such as *but*. The following list shows a move from the most colloquial (but) to the most literary and formal (whereas):

but; though; although; yet; while; whereas

Use the list to test the students: can they put them in order of formality (as in the list)?

Exercise 3 gives students further practice in using *unless* and *if not* in the form of a game.

3 Wishful thinking!

Exercise 4

The answers are:

A 1) **B** 2) **C** 3)

The students will already know that in Extracts **A** and **B,** there is the 'real' possibility of spending time reading more newspapers, or of Billy getting a camera. Also, they will probably know that it is now impossible to give Joe the programme on horseracing. However, this exercise focuses on a different aspect of the use of conditionals. Here, the most likely suggestions in terms of reality are the most unlikely to happen: Billy will never change the history of photography just by getting a camera. But the now impossible event – asking Joe – really would have happened if Ted Stenhouse had known about his interest in horses. There is therefore a difference between wishful thinking, and talking about missed but genuine opportunities.

Exercise 5: Free answers, suitable for homework.

Ask students to look at their answers to **2 Conditionals** in the 'Children talking' Doc Spot. Check how true or fanciful their answers were. As a further spoken or written exercise, students can extend their answers to **3 Writing** (from the same documentary) by imagining things they would do, if only they had . . . but which are wishful thinking.

4   Introducing conditions

This detailed exercise is designed to widen the students' vocabulary and range of styles.

Exercise 6

The answers are:

A	if only	**G**	unless
B	otherwise	**H**	in that case
C	if he'd known that	**I**	in case of complaint
D	he would probably	**J**	provided that
E	if you	**K**	if not
F	I hope you won't mind if	**L**	just imagine if

KEY WORDS AND PHRASES

Note the stress patterns associated with *photograph* apply to all words that end in *-ograph*:

   ocea'nographer;   car'tographer;   bi'ographer
   oceano'graphic;   carto'graphic;   bio'graphic

Give the students the following list of nouns, without stress markings, to see if they can predict the patterns:

A	phi'losophy	phi'losopher	philo'sophic
	ge'ology	ge'ologist	geo'logical
B	'democrat	de'mocracy	demo'cratic
	'family	fa'miliar	famili'arity
	'automat	au'tomaton	auto'matic

Words with similar structures normally follow the above patterns. Word stress is dealt with in more detail in Unit 15.

---
6   Pronunciation

UNIT 7

It's not as if...

Talking about conditions (2)

AIMS

The main aim of this unit is to make the students aware of the wide range of expressions associated with conditionality. This builds on Unit 6, and leads to a controlled but creative use of the new phrases in this unit.

PRE-VIEWING PREPARATION

SIT COM: **1 In the office**
                4 Fire in Sarah's flat

DOC SPOTS: **Town planning** reading passage and **1 Comprehension** (optional)

                Electricity reading passage and **1 Comprehension**

CONUNDRUM: **1 In the garage**

LANGUAGE REVIEW

In this unit you have extended your ability to talk about conditions, and you have practised

1 indicating that something worse might have happened:
   It's not as if it's broken.
   At least you're not hurt.

2 making a contrast using *even so, nevertheless, still, all the same, despite that,* and *in spite of that*:
   Even so, I haven't done any harm to the grass.

3 making a strong condition using *so long as, provided (that), on condition that* and *surely if*:
   So long as you don't set fire to it.

4 expressing degrees of certainty using *must have* and *might have*:
   John went home. (certain)
   John must have gone home. (less certain)
   John might have gone home. (uncertain)

KEY WORDS
AND PHRASES

an action

against the law

an apology

apparently

a cold

    to catch a cold

to commit

complex

a conflict

to consume (food or goods)

a crew

demolition

to destroy

to distribute

equipment

to exercise

to export

fantastic

the fire brigade

fish and chips

FOOD AND COOKING IN BRITAIN

Fish and chips are normally bought in fish and chip shops; if cooked at home, they taste different. British people cook food in pots and pans on stoves, which are electric or gas, or in ovens. The electric hotplates are sometimes called 'hobs'. Every house has a kettle for boiling water.

to fluctuate

a frying pan

generous

harm

to harm

healthy

illegal

immediate

irritating

a lead

a lifestyle

a local council

a micro/microcomputer

microcomputing

an occasion

an offence

piracy

to predict

a referendum

regulations

reliable

to repeat

to reproduce

a resident

serious

sympathy

tough

trade

training

unfair

a vicious circle

a videocassette

video piracy

a video recorder

video recording

a Visual Display Unit (VDU)

to warn

ER . . . ? IT'S . . . ER . . .

What's-his-name   ⎫
What's-her-name   ⎬ a person

a whatsit

a thingummy-bob ⎫
a thingamajig   ⎬ a thing
a doo-dah   ⎭

PHRASES

in the open air

I shall take no further action.

In this instance . . .

On condition that . . .

There's no harm in (doing) . . .

Give my regards to your wife!

It's all his fault!

Curtains! = the end (like when the final curtain falls at the end of a play in the theatre)

Its curtains for him. = It's the end for him.

 SIT COM

1 In the office

All the things listed are possibilities for people who want to keep fit. Apart from teaching the expressions, the guide also practises the students' powers of observation. Teach the contents of the guide before playing the sequence. Ask the students for their opinions first: which things on the list do they think that Billy will do? Compare their suggestions with what he actually does. Play the scene without sound first. Replay the scene as necessary until the whole class have the correct answers.

The answers are:

A, B, D, F, G

2 In the canteen

This is a controlled exercise in sequencing. Use the same technique, but without supplying any cues, with the scene about Ted parking his car: play the scene several times, and ask the students to write an account of what happened. This revises the use of past tense forms.

3 In the park

The park regulations look obscure. They have developed over the years, and each of the byelaws probably reflects some habit or practice that once caused a nuisance.

London is famous for the number of green spaces in the city. There are two reasons for the large number of parks, both historical. In the city centre, there are many expensive town houses in squares. The houses were built around a green open area of gardens or trees to provide an area of relaxation exclusive to the residents of the square. Many of these squares have now become town council property. The large parks, such as Hyde Park, were originally royal hunting parks. As they are still owned by the Crown, they have escaped destruction and town development.

4 Fire in Sarah's flat

Prepare the vocabulary before playing the sequence. The students need to understand the dialogue about the fire to benefit from Language Study **1 It's not as if . . .**, **At least . . .** . With some classes, it may be preferable to teach the Language Study section before watching the sequence.

The answers are:
The kitchen is almost totally destroyed.
The sitting room is badly damaged.
The bedrooms are ruined by water.

5 Who was it?

Do not prepare this with the students. They may be surprised at how few (or how many) adequate descriptions they can give. The person who walks in is Sarah, wearing a grey/blue jumpsuit.

6 Ted's manner

The scene can be played without sound, so that the students can estimate how many changes of mood there are. With sound and vision, the students can match Ted's manner to the texts given. The sentences teach new vocabulary, extending the adjectives to adverbs.

The correct order is: **A, E, C, D, B**

D⦿ DOC SPOT 1　Town planning

Present the text as standard, and then watch the Doc Spot.

1　Comprehension

The comprehension questions can be completed before or after viewing: it may be useful to prepare the questions first, view twice, and then attempt to answer the questions.

The answers are:

A ✕　B √　C ✕　D √　E ✕　F √　G √　H ✕

2　Reported and direct speech

This revises the contents of Language Study **2 Reported speech** in Unit 5.

The answers are:

A　Mr Tilley said that most of the buildings in the centre would be pulled down.
B　Mr Tilley said that the proposals would provide for new shops.
C　'There has been opposition.' (Mr Tilley)
D　Mr Tilley said that trade in the town centre would continue to decline.
E　Mr Thwaite said that they (the residents) were against large-scale demolition.
F　'I want to see a referendum.' (Mr Thwaite)

3　For and against

The arguments marshalled by the students can be used in a classroom debate. They can also form the basis of written assignments for homework or private study: the notes must be turned into a coherent text.

Some possible arguments are:

FOR THE NEW PROPOSALS	AGAINST THE NEW PROPOSALS
– new shops – bring people to Wimbledon – stop the decline in trade – increase trade – give Wimbledon a secure future	– large-scale demolition of attractive Victorian and Edwardian streets – new roads bring more cars and traffic – Wimbledon will become more built-up, with fewer green, open spaces – office blocks will make the centre of Wimbledon ugly – the proposals will change the character of the area

4　Planning

Some groups may need help to draw a plan. Any town may be chosen, basing the alternatives on town plans available locally, or on plans that students may have bought when travelling around their own country or abroad.

D⦿ DOC SPOT 2　Electricity

1　Comprehension

Present the text and the comprehension questions as standard. When the students are familiar with the topic and key vocabulary, play the Doc Spot.

The answers are:

A A system for transmitting electricity to all consumers in England and Wales.
B No. It is impossible to store electricity in large amounts.
C It increases the demand for electricity.
D It is transferred by overhead cables.
E When the temperature drops the demand goes up.
F From the Weather Centre in Bracknell.

 1 Listening comprehension

2 Increasing and reducing demand

This is an easy exercise in establishing cause and effect.

The answers are:

A Heavy rain increases the demand for umbrellas.
B A high birthrate increases the demand for nursery schools.
C Advertising increases the demand for new cars.
D Hot weather increases the demand for ice cream.
E Cold weather decreases the demand for bathing costumes.
F Price rises decrease the demand for consumer goods.

The exercise can be made more difficult by asking the class to rewrite the sentences, using this model:

An increase in demand for umbrellas is usually caused by heavy rain.

 2 Drill

3 Pair work

If a cold winter is not suitable for local conditions, then get the class to choose a suitable alternative, eg ten ways to save water during an extended drought; ten precautions to take in preparation for imminent floods.
Free answers.

4 What's the problem?

The puzzle promotes intensive reading of the text.

The answers are:

A store
B consumer
C increase
D transmit

E demand
F megawatt
G amount
H predict

The key word is 'powercut' – when there is a breakdown in the transmission of electricity to consumers.

5 Electricity project

There may well be members of the class who know this information.
Make them group leaders for the development of group projects.

 CONUNDRUM

1 In the garage

At last the secret of the garage is revealed! The students need to appreciate how much Mrs Gibbs really knows for a better understanding of later parts of the plot. Be sure they answer the questions without looking ahead.

The answers are:

A × B √ C × D × E √ F × G √ H √ I √ J ×

2 Discussing the case

The left-hand column contains colloquial items. *What's-his-name*, the way of referring to somebody one knows but whose name one has forgotten, is followed up in the **Key words and phrases.**

The answers are:

A 4) B 1) C 2) D 5) E 3)

3 Mrs Taylor's story

If the students do not guess that the spot is the grave of a dog, give them clues: point out that it is a grave, but in a private garden, and that only one first name is given, rather than a full name. A dog is often referred to in English as 'man's best friend'.

---

3 Who said it?

LANGUAGE STUDY

1 It's not as if . . ., At least . . .

The key difference between the phrases *at least* . . . and *it's not as if* . . . lies in the fact that *at least* . . . does not affect the truth or likelihood of the following statement. It merely shows the speaker's attitude to the statement. *It's not as if* . . . is part of the whole statement; it denies that what is asserted took place.

NB *It's as if* . . . tells the listener that the speaker imagines that something has happened.

Note that the expression *'look on the bright side'* is used in the Students' Book. Students should remember this from 'Conundrum' in Unit 2.

Exercises 1 and 2 are rather mechanical, as the students need to practise the meanings and syntax before the more open-ended exercises with the cue cards in Exercise 3.

The answers to Exercise 1 are:

A At least you're not too late.
B At least you haven't broken any bones.
C At least you've got some money left.
D At least the bedrooms weren't ruined.
E It's not as if you've been injured.
F It's not as if you won't be able to attend the meeting.
G It's not as if you will have to pay for everything.
H It's not as if you're not safe.

---

4 Drill

---

2   So long as . . ., Even so . . .

The terms *even so, so long as, all the same* and *still* are the most colloquial of those listed. The others are more formal or suited to written text.

The answers are:
EVEN SO: nevertheless, still, despite that, in spite of that, all the same
SO LONG AS: provided that, on condition, surely if

The answers to Exercise 2 are:

A Even so, I'm still trying to keep fit.

B Even so, I enjoy reading Kurt Vonnegut's books.

C So long as you agree, we'll go to Italy for our holiday.

D So long as it rains, there'll be enough water to fill the pond.

E Even so, I'd like to have a look at it myself.

Exercise 3

Allow the class plenty of time to prepare notes for their pair work negotiations. Cue cards **A2** and **B2** are on p168 of the Students' Book.

Two sets of cue cards are included:

Set **A1/A2** – Speaker **A1** begins with positive sentences:

'If you lend me the money, I'll . . .'

'If you lent me the money, I'd . . .'

Speaker **A2** must respond with negatives sentences.

Set **B1/B2** – Speaker **B1** begins with negative sentences:

'If you don't lend me the . . ., I won't be able to . . .'

'If you don't lend me the . . ., I can't . . .'

Speaker **B2** must respond with negative sentences.

Use the cue cards with the class as shown. Then return to them at a later date, asking **A** pairs to be **B**s, and **B** pairs to be **A**s.

Encourage fantasy and role play throughout the exercise: the livelier the better.

3   Degrees of certainty in the past

Exercise 4

The clues in brackets will help students choose the right answer.
The answers are:

A Sue might have been to Germany.

B Anne must have been to France.

C He might have given up (smoking).

D Jim might have gone swimming.

E He must have read that book/it.

   5   Drill

KEY WORDS AND PHRASES

Curtains! and *It's curtains for him!* are colloquial and would normally be used in an informal situation.

   6   Pronunciation

UNIT 8

The police were called...

Using the passive

AIMS

The main aim of this unit is to consolidate the students' use of the passive in English. Some common phrasal verbs are also presented and studied.

PRE-VIEWING PREPARATION

SIT COM: **1 In Pierre's restaurant**
            3 Men can't do anything

DOC SPOTS: **Learning languages** reading passage

            Acid rain reading passage and **1 Comprehension** (optional)

CONUNDRUM: **1 The neighbour**
            2 Mr Hutchinson – suspect

LANGUAGE REVIEW

In this unit you have practised using different forms of the passive in English. You have learnt that

1 some sentences never require an agent to be mentioned:

   The police were called.

   My watch is being repaired.

2 if an action is the cause of something, then you use the *by -ing* construction:

   My life has been transformed by coming here.

   My health has improved greatly by drinking Vito-Cee.

3 and you have looked at phrasal verbs, made up of verbs with prepositions and adverbs:

   We'll be coming back. Don't go away from home. Please get in.

KEY WORDS
AND PHRASES

to adore
an advantage
amazing
architecture
to break into
a bunch
to cancel
convenient
to convince

to defeat
defiant
a difficulty
to disappoint
to drop out
to exchange
exhaust fumes
to experience
to exploit

a factory
to fall behind
fascinating
to filter
to be fond of
a fossil
fuel
goodness
hardly
a health club
historic
to impress
to improve
incompetent
inefficient
to inform
   to keep informed
to install
to insult
to invite out
to iron
to jog
a label
a language laboratory
a limitation
in the meantime
muscles
to organise
the pain barrier
pre-arranged
a principle
a resource

to get round to
a script
a series
shocked
sinister
to smash
a snack
a spaniel
to transform
a tutorial

GUITO THE UNIT	▷ SIT COM

GUIDE TO THE UNIT

▷ SIT COM

1   In Pierre's restaurant

By working through the contents of the viewing guide before watching the sequence, the students will be prepared for the possibly difficult dialogue.

The answers are:

A ×   B √   C ×   D √   E √   F √   G ×   H √

1   Drill

2   Health clubs

The short conversation between Joe and Billy about health clubs is followed up by a longer sequence later in the unit.

The answers are: Joe √   fat executives √

3   Men can't do anything

Before you show this sequence, ask the students to guess the answers. Compare their guesses with what is really said.

The answer is: Prodip says he can cook.

4   At the health club

This is suitable for groups of 4 or 5, and can be used as a basis for a class debate.

D◉ DOC SPOT 1   Learning languages

Prepare the text as standard. When the students understand the topic, play the Doc Spot.

1   Comprehension

The comprehension activity can be used as a revision exercise in intensive reading.

The answers are:

A ×   B √   C √   D ×   E ×   F ×   G √

2   Listening comprehension
The answer is 'constant repetition'.

2   Timetable

The students can of course construct their own timetables as an extension of this exercise, and invent their own queries.

The answers are:

A There is a class on Monday and Friday at 8 pm and on Wednesday at 6 pm.
B Yes, there is a class on Monday and Friday at 7 pm and on Wednesday at 8 pm.
C There is a class on Monday and Friday at 9 pm and on Wednesday at 6 pm.
D Yes, there is a class on Monday and Friday at 6 pm and on Wednesday at 7 pm.
E There is a class on Wednesday at 8 pm and on Monday at 9 pm but the Friday class is at 6 pm.
F I'm sorry, there are no Spanish Advanced classes this year.

3 Project

Alternatively, this task can be related to a local college.

4 Puzzle

Extend the puzzle by asking more questions about countries and languages. For example, do the students know any other countries where these languages are spoken, or do they know what other languages are spoken in the countries listed?

The answers are:

A English	**E** Russian	**H** Turkish
B Swahili	**F** Arabic	**I** Portuguese
C Spanish	**G** Norwegian	**Key word** Esperanto
D German		

5 Choices

Students can choose any other language.

D⦿ DOC SPOT 2 Acid rain

Present the text as standard. When the students are familiar with the topic, play the Doc Spot.

1 Comprehension

The comprehension questions are suitable for a pre-viewing exercise or for homework.

The answers are:

A oil, coal, gas

B Fossil fuels contain sulphur. When they are burnt they form sulphuric acid.

C Pollution is carried there from other countries by the wind.

D Lakes become acidic and the fish disappear. Trees are eventually killed by acid rain.

E No, for example, Britain has not yet taken any really effective measures.

2 Follow the ecological disaster

This exercise helps to prepare the students for the exercises on using the passive and on sequencing in Language Study **1 The police were called**. It is suitable for private study, pair work or homework.

3 The acid rain problem

This task can be turned into a project on acid rain. If English language articles or features are not available, then students can use material in their own language as a source for facts which they must talk about in English.

As an extension exercise, present the students with headlines from English language newspaper articles on contentious environmental issues. These can be used as a basis for further class discussion which can lead into project work. Are there any local instances of industry polluting the environment?

 CONUNDRUM

1 The neighbour

The main purpose of this guide is to ensure the students appreciate that Mrs Taylor frequently heard shouting from the Gibbs' house.

The answers are:

Jack occasionally went into the Gibbs' garden.

He damaged the Gibbs' car once.

Mrs Taylor frequently heard shouting.

2 Mr Hutchinson – suspect

The first part of the guide gives the students the necessary vocabulary to talk about Hutchinson. The second part allows them to follow Hutchinson's testimony. The students need to understand what Hutchinson says in order to move on to the discussion task.

The answers are:

A × (they do not yet know all the details) **B** × **C** √ **D** √ **E** × **F** ×
G √ **H** √ **I** × **J** ×

3 Discussion

This exercise is suitable for discussion in groups of 4 or 5. Each group can decide who they think had the best motive and opportunity, and compare their chief suspect with those of other groups.

LANGUAGE STUDY

1 The police were called . . .

Note that the following forms of the passive are in italics in the Students' Book:

past perfect	*had been smashed*
present perfect	*has been broken into*
past simple	*were called*
	were given
present continuous	*is being repaired*

The use of tense forms in this extract follows on from the explanations of tenses given in the Language Study sections of Units 4 and 5.

Exercise 1

This exercise draws the attention of the students to the fact that passive sentences in English are usually composed in the passive. They do not start as active sentences which are transposed to the passive.

The only way that the students can answer the questions set is to use common sense. The text does not carry the answers.

Exercise 2

This gives students the opportunity to practice forming the passive. In contrast to Exercise 1, this exercise shows how the passive voice can be used for effect. Notice how the mystery of **D** in enhanced when the passive is used. Authors often use the passive for dramatic effect.

The answers are:

A The window has been closed.

B My tape recorder has been broken.

C I am being met at the station at eight.

D The door was opened slowly, but there was no one in sight.

E My handbag has been stolen!

Exercise 3

Instruct the class to write the text as a letter of complaint, starting perhaps with:

Dear Sir,
I am writing to complain about the hi-fi system which I bought from the shop
(Exquisite Sounds) last week.
The unit was unpacked following the . . .

Note that the first and last verbs in the exercise (*read* and *enjoy*) should not be put into passive forms in the letter.

2   You'll be amazed by the difference!

Students should appreciate that most verbs can be used as a noun, merely by adding *–ing* to the main verb. This also applies to phrasal verbs:

by going away = by leaving
by coming back = by returning (See **3 Phrasal verbs**)

Exercise 4

Sample answers are:

A My health has been improved by drinking Vito-Cee.

B I discovered new adventures by spending my holiday in Cornwall.

C My memory has been improved by studying the Mnemo home course.

D I became a financial genius by enrolling at the Mammon business school.

E I learned to read faster by using the Lexico Rapid Reading Systems.

 5   Drill

Exercise 5

Free answers, suitable for private study and then group discussion.

3   Phrasal verbs

The prepositions listed will be known to the students. Most phrasal verbs with prepositions cannot be split:

The mayor *ran for* President (= stood for election as)
The house owner *laid into* the burglars (= attacked)

The adverbs listed can form phrasal verbs which are better split:

He *brought* the couple *together.* (= introduced them)
He *took* his friends *aside.*

They can also form phrasal verbs which cannot be split:

He *came to* in the hospital. (= regained consciousness)
Her argument *runs counter* to modern thinking.

Exercise 6

This can eventually be used as a basis for a quiz where students ask each other the meanings of phrasal verbs they have found. Students can also be encouraged to make up sentences using phrasal verbs in context, or to illustrate the meanings of the verbs by drawing cartoon pictures.

The lists in the Students' Book can be supplemented by the following:

verbs	prepositions	adverbs	prepositions & adverbs
to be	ahead of	abreast	above
to call	astride	abroad	alongside
to cut	beneath	adrift	around
to do	like	aground	below
to draw	on top of	aloft	between
to fall		astray	beyond
to have		backwards	inside
to keep		downhill	outside
to knock		downstairs	round
to look		forward(s)	under
to pass		home	underneath
to pull		indoors	without
to sit		in front	
to stand		on top	
to stick		overboard	
to throw		underground	
to turn		upstairs	

KEY WORDS AND PHRASES

Note the construction *That's because . . .* , used by Mrs Belmont to introduce her reason:

Joe:	Mrs Belmont, can I ask you something?
	Why's the sugar kept in the coffee can and the coffee kept in the sugar can?
Mrs Belmont:	Oh, that's because the labels are wrong.
Joe:	Oh, right.
Mrs Belmont:	I've always meant to change them but never got round to it.

That's stands in place of the whole problem:

The sugar is kept in the coffee can and the coffee is kept in the sugar can because . . .

That's is normally stressed. If there is no emphasis, then *it's* can be used.

UNIT 9

Because, since, due to ...

Expressing cause and effect

AIMS   This unit focuses on linking language to express cause and effect, with register and appropriacy as the secondary theme. There is also extended practice in talking about and describing people and their reactions.

PRE-VIEWING PREPARATION

SIT COM:	**1 Prodip the musician**
	2 Ted's apology
DOC SPOTS:	**Making bells** reading passage
	Mount St Helens reading passage and **1 Comprehension**
CONUNDRUM:	Prepare key vocabulary

LANGUAGE REVIEW

In this unit you have learnt

1 some words and phrases to express cause and effect and to give reasons:
   as, as a result (of), because (of), consequently, due to, owing to, since, so, therefore

2 when to use the appropriate language:
   I must ask you to . . . (formal)
   Could you . . .? (less formal, but still polite)

3 how to ask someone to do something:
   Would you mind turning on the television, please? (very polite)
   Could you turn on the television, please? (polite)
   Can you turn on the television, please? (to a friend)

4 You have also extended your ability to describe people:
   He was a tallish man in his late twenties, with ginger hair, wearing an ankle-length leather coat and a beret.

KEY WORDS AND PHRASES

absurd
an accident
actually
aggressive
to agree
appropriate
ash
to assume
available
to avoid
to brake
brakes
   to put on one's brakes
careless driving
carelessness
to cause

chimes (of a bell)
a concert hall
consequently
to contact
to be in contact with
convection
to deal with
a defender
to devastate
a disaster
a drought

erratic
to erupt
an eruption
experienced
to export
a flood
flooded
to force
to be forced to
a foundry
generally
to go through
to be held up
handwriting
hemisphere
ignorance
innocent
justice
a landmark
laziness
to lift
to melt
molten
a mood
a mould
nervous
nuclear bombs
of course
to pick up
a pleasure
pressure
to presume
to put on
a reaction
to realise
to repeat
to report someone for
   something

a scientist
to share
sideways
a situation
skilled
to skim
slippers
stratosphere
stupidity
to suffer from shock
to suggest
to tune
to turn up
unforeseen
   an unforeseen difficulty
unjust
unprecedented
urgent
a volcano
a washing machine

PHRASES
to throw a spanner in the works
out of a sense of obligation . . .
There is more to life than . . .
You were bound to . . .
He was bound to . . . (+ verb)
He was forced to . . . (+ verb)
That gives rise to . . . (+ noun)
This is due to . . . (+ noun)

SIT COM

1 Prodip the musician

This easy task of identifying what Prodip is doing serves two purposes:

- – it prepares the students for the group discussion, which may take place after the whole unit has been watched
- – it sets up the students' expectations about Ted's reactions.

The answer is:

Prodip is conducting music and playing a record.

2 Ted's apology

This type of hyperbolic irony is typical of one style of English humour.

Students select their own answers.

 1 Drill

3 Ted's washing machine

Answer: Prodip
Notice Prodip's riposte, also using irony:
Prodip: That's all right. I enjoy lifting washing machines.

4 Billy, the office boy

Interpreting Sarah's behaviour is an extension of the activity in **2 Ted's apology**.

Students select their own answers.

5 In the canteen

Joe is momentarily puzzled: he thinks Mrs Belmont is referring to him when she says 'black'. In fact, she is referring to the coffee and is asking if he would like his coffee black or white.

6 The car crash

The dialogue in this scene is treated extensively in the Language Study section.
The answers are:
A Ted   B Ted   C Woman   D Woman   E Woman   F Ted   G Ted   H Ted

D◉ DOC SPOT 1   Making bells

Present the text as standard. When the students understand the topic, play the Doc Spot.

1 Comprehension

The comprehension exercise can be kept as an activity to be completed after viewing.
The answers are:
A moulds
B mould, baked
C mould, inner
D molten metal, space (*or* gap)
E outer mould, is tuned (*or* is cleaned prior to tuning)
F skimmed (*or* scraped)

2 The bell-making process

This activity follows up the main teaching point of Unit 8, the use of the passive.

The answers are:

A 4) **B** 7) **C** 1) **D** 2) **E** 6) **F** 3) **G** 5)

3 Project

The answers are:

A an Egyptian obelisk on the Thames Embankment –
The twin to Cleopatra's needle is in the centre of Paris, France.

B a monument commemorating the fire of London (1666) –
The fire of London is believed to have started in Pudding Lane, in the City of London. The height of the monument is also the distance of the monument from the shop where the fire started.

C a royal castle near Tower Bridge –
The Tower has been a palace, a prison and a museum at various times since 1078.

D a corner of Hyde Park –
Speakers' Corner is at its most active on Sundays at about midday. Some of the views expressed there are very extreme; some are very amusing. Most speakers welcome interruptions from hecklers in the crowd.

E an East London Sunday market –
Petticoat Lane is very difficult to find on the street maps of London, as the official name for the road is Middlesex Street. Note that in street names, the word *Street* is never stressed:
'Oxford Street, 'Middlesex Street.
If there is another word (eg Road, Lane, Avenue) then there is level stress:
'Petticoat 'Lane, 'Shaftesbury 'Avenue, 'London 'Road
Word stress is studied in detail in Unit 15.

F a memorial to Queen Victoria's husband in Kensington Gardens –
Prince Albert of Saxe-Coburg-Gotha (1819–1861) was the husband of Queen Victoria; she reigned until 1901, having ascended the throne in 1837.

G a cathedral in the City –
St Paul's Cathedral was built by Sir Christopher Wren, a brilliant mathematician and engineer, who helped reconstruct London after the Great Fire. On the floor of the cathedral, under the great dome, is an inscription dedicated to Wren. In Latin, it says *Si monumentum requiris circumspice.* (If you seek my monument, then look around you.)

H a statue in Trafalgar Square –
The column was put up to honour Lord Horatio Nelson, killed at the Battle of Trafalgar in 1805.

I a statue at Piccadilly Circus –
The statue of Eros was unveiled in 1893; it was the first statue in London to be made of aluminium. It is a memorial to the Earl of Shaftesbury, a noted philanthropist. Eros is the God of Love; the statue was originally intended to represent the Angel of Christian Charity.

J where the Buckingham Palace horses and carriages are kept –
The Royal Mews are used to house the Queen's 30 horses, 70 carriages, and 20 motor cars (latest available figures). In many parts of London, the original mews behind large houses have been converted from stables to small but expensive and fashionable residences.

4 Find the connection

A bell-ringing – a bell-tower is also called a campanile

B invented by Alexander Graham Bell (1847–1922) – a Scotsman who emigrated to America

C pen-name 'Ellis Bell' – all three Brontë sisters used the nom de plume Bell: Anne was Acton Bell and Charlotte was Currer Bell

D bell-ringer of Notre Dame in Victor Hugo's novel – Hugo wrote *Notre Dame de Paris* in 1831. The character who in the story grows up to be the notorious hunchback of Notre Dame is found by nuns as a baby on the morning of Low Sunday, the first Sunday after Easter in the Christian church calendar. The first prayer for that day is, in Latin, *Quasi modo geniti infantes* (As is the way of newborn babies . . .), so the foundling child received the name *Quasimodo*.

E a bell is rung when the last lap begins

D DOC SPOT 2   Mount St Helens

1   Comprehension

Present the text and comprehension questions as standard. When the class understand the topic, play the Doc Spot.

The answers are:

A erupt

B unprecedented

C convection

D drought

E flood

F erratic

Note that *Mount* is often abbreviated to *Mt.*

Other common abbreviations for place names are:

Ave – Avenue	Pk – Park
Bldgs – Buildings	Pl – Place
Cres – Crescent	Rd – Road
Ct – Court	Sq – Square
Est – Estate	St – Street
Gdns – Gardens	Stn – Station
Gt – Great	Ter – Terrace
Pal – Palace	Yd – Yard

Ask students what these are short for:

Buck Pal Rd   (Buckingham Palace Road)
Tot Ct Rd   (Tottenham Court Road)
Warren St Stn (Warren Street Station)

---

 2   Drill

---

2   Definitions

This activity can be used for group work, for homework or for private study.

The answers are:

A gale
hurricane
cyclone

B earthquake
earth tremor

C avalanche
(= landslide if not ice or snow)

D tornado
whirlwind

E flood

F tidal wave

---

 3   Drill

---

3 Project

This is a further opportunity for encyclopaedia and project work. This activity can be kept in reserve for use later in the unit or for homework.

The answers are:

Vesuvius (Italy), Fuji (Japan), Popocatepetl (Mexico), and Etna (Sicily) are all volcanoes.
The Matterhorn is in Switzerland, Mont Blanc is on the French/Swiss border. Mount Everest is the highest mountain in the world, and is in the Himalayas. Mount Rushmore is in the USA, and has the faces of presidents carved on the front.

 CONUNDRUM

1 Mr Hutchinson – suspect

A This activity focuses the students' attention both on Hutchinson's alibi, and on their own ability to describe people in English. Play the flashbacks and ask students to fill out the form working on their own, then ask them to compare their descriptions in groups. Finally, play the scene again and see who has the most accurate description.

B You see Alec Lee, Bernie Raistrick, Felicity Curran and Mr Hutchinson.

2 Bernie Raistrick – chief steward

A Raistrick's manner can be interpreted in many ways. Towards the end of 'Conundrum', his role in the story becomes more important. The students should therefore be led to concentrate on him now, but without suspecting anything about his future importance.

The answers are:
A 4)   **B** 1)   **C** 5)   **D** 3)   **E** 2)

B Free answers, suitable for group or class discussion.

---

 4 Drill

---

3 Mrs Taylor – Gibbs' neighbour

This develops the students' ideas about Raistrick – if they make the right assumptions. Do not confirm who Gibbs argued with.

LANGUAGE STUDY

1 Because, since, due to . . .

The extended quote from the scene of Ted's crash is used again as the text for the appropriacy exercise.

Exercise 1

The answers are:

A constitute
B therefore, that's why, as a result
C because of, the result of, owing to
D as, because
E therefore

F in order to, so that I could
G therefore, as a result of which, as a result
H cause, result in

Exercise 2

When volcanoes blow out upwards, they shoot dust and gas into the stratosphere. *As a result*, the material blocks out heat from the sun. *Consequently*, the earth gets colder, *and* the effect of convection – which makes hot air rise – is suppressed. *Therefore*, the circulation doesn't work properly *and* everything changes. There are droughts and floods and so on. *Sometimes* this lasts for about two or three years. Luckily, Mount St Helens blew out sideways *so* the dust had little effect.

2 Giving reasons

Exercise 3

Further examples of instructions can be given to the students for project work. They can take examples from material published in their own language if instructions in English are not available. Encourage students to use cause and effect connecting words from Language Study 1.

3 What is appropriate?

This builds on Unit 5, Language Study 3.

Exercise 4

Possible answers are:

1) are causing an obstruction
2) consequently
3) I must ask you to

4) may I suggest that
5) in my experience
6) give rise to

Exercise 5

Substitute the words listed for the words in Exercise 4.

4 Asking someone to do something

Exercise 6

Possible answers are:

A Can you help me?
B Would you mind if I took the afternoon off to go to the dentist?
C Could you tell me the way to the nearest bank, please?
D Would you mind making less noise?
E Could you make out my bill, please?

Note that *'Could you . . .?'* is the most frequently used form.

6 Drill

KEY WORDS AND PHRASES

–less, –ness, and *–lessness* can be added to many, but not all, nouns.

Some common affixes which change the class of words are:

a–	changes verbs to particles: aboard, aground
be–	changes nouns to verbs: befriend
	changes adjectives to verbs: belittle
en–	changes adjectives to verbs: enrich, enlarge
	changes nouns to verbs: enslave
–tion	changes verbs to nouns: education
–al	changes nouns to adjectives: educational, habitual
–ise	changes adjectives to verbs: rationalise

The advertisements for the well-known Irish beer, Guinness, draw on the apparent structure of the word to invent a concept of *being without a Guinness: Guinnesslessness,* or *Guinnlessness.*

UNIT 10

It's as simple as ABC!

Making comparisons

AIMS

The main aim of this unit is to consolidate the students' use of the various expressions in English for comparing people and things. The exercises based on the Sit Com offer group discussion activities using comparatives and superlatives, whilst the Language Study section gives the students an analysis of some of the more difficult expressions used in the unit.

PRE-VIEWING PREPARATION

SIT COM:
1 The cinema
2 In the office
3 In the guitar shop

DOC SPOTS:
Tea reading passage and **1 Comprehension**
Synthesisers reading passage and **1 Comprehension**

CONUNDRUM:
1 Felicity Curran – Hutchinson's alibi
2 Felicity Curran – witness
3 Alec Lee – suspect

LANGUAGE REVIEW

In this unit you have consolidated your knowledge of expressions for comparing things in English:

1 using *as . . . as . . .*
   It's as simple as ABC.
   I don't play as well as I'd like to.

2 using dependent comparatives:
   The sooner, the better.
   The less you pay, the less you get.

3 using modifiers of adjectives:
   It's fairly expensive.
   It's quite nice.
   It's good enough for me.

4 using modifiers of comparative adjectives:
   I want something a great deal cheaper.
   It's just a little better than rubbish.
   The tone is much richer.

5 You have also practised forming adjectives and adverbs as comparatives and superlatives:

adjective/adverb	comparative	superlative
cheap	cheaper	cheapest
sophisticated	more sophisticated	most sophisticated
badly	worse	worst
little	less	least
much	more	most

KEY WORDS
AND PHRASES

absolute
an accountant
to affect
the age of the . . .
alone
altitude
an artist
to assess
an auction
a beginner
to break someone's alibi
brittle
a can of film
climate
a commodity
to compare
complex
complicated
to compose
to consider
considerable
a crop
a customer
to demonstrate
to depend on
to dominate
dried
elaborate
elusive
an estate
expertise
extremely

FILM, VIDEO, CABLE
Hollywood is the famous centre of the cinema industry, where multi-million dollar movies are made. But film has many rivals today, including videotapes and cable television.

fairly
a flavour
a fluctuation
to have fun with
furious
a guitar
idiotic
indistinguishable
intense
an invention
a key witness
leading
main
middle-aged
moisture
a movie

MUSICIANS
Musicians play instruments, or compose, or conduct.
There are ordinary players and artists. A few are recognised as a 'maestro' or as a 'virtuoso'.

to be musical
a mystic
an offer

an orchestra
origin
a particle
a perfectionist
pessimistic
to play the guitar
to pluck
pretentious
the Prime Minister
to process
a producer
realistic
to reduce
to reproduce
to require
romantic
rubbish
scared
to sell in bulk
simple
slightly
sophisticated
a string orchestra
a studio
sweet
sympathetic
a synthesiser
to taste
a tea taster
a threat
a valuation
to value
various
virtually
wise

▷ SIT COM

Language Study 3 contains a listening task that requires sections of the Sit Com to be shown for note-taking purposes.

It may be useful to splice the Language Study activities into the viewing guides in this section.

An overview of the comparison of adjectives is given in this manual in the Language Study section.

1 The cinema

Prepare the contents of the discussion guide before showing the sequence, so that the students can follow what is being said.

Free answers, suitable for group or class discussion.

2 In the office

The students can extend their vocabulary by making up similar mix-and-match puzzles, using a good dictionary.

The answers are:

A 3) **B** 4) **C** 2) **D** 1)

3 In the guitar shop

Prepare the language in the viewing guide first. Note that *absolute* is being used to qualify *rubbish*. If an adjective is being modified, then absolute*ly* is used: *It's absolutely awful!*

The answers are:

– much too expensive, expensive, a bit more expensive, not that expensive, a great deal cheaper, extremely cheap

– quite good, good enough, not bad, quite bad, rubbish, absolute rubbish

---

   1 Stress   Prepare the students for this audio exercise with spoken examples of how stress can alter the meaning of an utterance.

D⦿ DOC SPOT 1   Tea

1 Comprehension

Present the text as standard, and complete the comprehension questions as a pre-viewing exercise. When the students understand the topic, play the Doc Spot.

The answers are:

the climate (√), where it is grown (√),
the part of the bush (√), the day it is plucked (√)

---

   2 Drill

---

2 One nation, one drink

Note that the makers of quality teas are more insistent about the length of time needed for the tea to draw.

The correct order is:

B, F, D, C, H, E, A, G

British people claim that one of the secrets of good tea is that the water must be actually boiling when the tea is made – not just very hot. Almost every British household has a kettle which is only used for boiling water. It is very unusual indeed to take water for tea from a water heater, or from water heated on the stove in a saucepan. Similarly, the teapot is only used for tea. If there are other drinks made in the house, such as coffee or cocoa, then separate pots or jugs are used.

3   Listen for detail

3   Job maker

Most trades or professions are carried out by people whose descriptions end in –er or –or:

teacher, learner, solicitor, professor, photographer

Many, however, end in –nt, –ian, or –ist:

student, assistant, technician, dentist, physicist

A person who is good at a variety of things involving manual skills (such as carpentry, plumbing and so on) is called a 'handyman'. Someone who can do anything is a 'Jack-of-all-trades'.

The answers are:

A a person who collects fares on a bus
B a person who sells books
C a person who makes money (takes bets) on, eg horse races (a bookie)
D a person who owns or manages a shop
E a person who steals goods from shops
F a person who watches wild birds in their natural surroundings
G a person who while at work watches the clock all day waiting for the time he or she can go home
H a person who sweeps the road
I a person who is in charge of a department in a large shop or store (senior sales person)
J a person who smuggles guns and firearms

4   Words of the alphabet

The class may like to compose sentences from single letters and numbers; for example, *RU 18?* is a sign which asks teenagers whether they are old enough to drink in a pub: *Are you eighteen?*

The answers are:
A bee   B see   C sea   D eye   E owe   F pea   G queue   H you

5   Things that go with tea

Tea leaves are kept in the tea caddy (usually a tin or square wooden box). When the tea is made, it is kept warm in the pot by a tea cosy, and may be served from a tea trolley with tea biscuits or cake, all neatly arranged on a tea set (crockery). When the time comes for the washing up, the tea set is dried on a tea towel.

D◉ DOC SPOT 2   Synthesisers

1   Comprehension

Present the text and comprehension questions as standard. When the students understand the topic, play the Doc Spot.

Possible answers are:

A the guitar

B No, the synthesiser has taken its place.

C an elaborate electric piano

D It can reproduce the sound of almost any real instrument and it can memorise and replay pieces of music.

E 'play' all the instruments wanted to make a record

F the inventor of the first music synthesiser

G a Visual Display Unit

H A synthesiser produces a sound which is almost as good as a real orchestra.

2 Looks like/feels like

The answers are:

A sounds like	E feels like	H feels like
B smells	F sounds like	I looks like
C looks like	G tastes like	J feels/looks
D tastes like		

4 Drill

When verbs such as *look* or *see* are used in the continuous form, their meanings are changed from the primary meaning of senses to a secondary meaning:
I'm seeing the doctor tomorrow = I'm visiting the doctor tomorrow.

Use the following to ask the class about secondary meanings or primary meanings in various contexts:

1) I'm sounding out the committee next week.

2) I'm not feeling very well.

3) You're looking good today!

4) We are going to a wine tasting session.

3 Synthesisers and the future

The discussion can be related to the role of pop, rock and folk music in the students' own country/countries.

 CONUNDRUM

1 Felicity Curran – Hutchinson's alibi

Make sure the students understand the exercise before they view the sequence.
The answer is: **B** √

In Britain the use of names, and the laws concerning names, are more relaxed than in many countries.
Most women, when they marry, take the surname of their husband.
For example, if Mary Cartwright marries Thomas Clark, she becomes Mary Clark. In formal circles, a wife may be addressed by her husband's first name: Mrs Thomas Clark. However, this practice is dying out.
A woman can keep her own name if she wishes. Many professional women keep their maiden name for business purposes. The abbreviation 'Ms' is now used by many women in Britain rather than 'Miss' or 'Mrs'. The usual way of showing both a married and a maiden name is to use the French expression *née* (= born as): Mary Clark, née Cartwright. There is no law in Britain which prevents any person calling

himself or herself by any name he or she likes. A person can just write to the bank, the employer and other interested people, and say 'From now on, I would like to be known as James King.' The only legal requirement is that the change must not be for deception or other illegal purposes.

2   Felicity Curran – witness

This is an important sequence, as it establishes who apparently had a chance to kill Gibbs. Read through the exercise with the students before viewing the sequence.

The answers are:
A   1) in the foyer   2) outside the lift
B   the airline pilot and the chief steward
C   between 7 and 8

3   Alec Lee – suspect

This leads into the discussion activity in **5 Discussion**. Make sure the students understand the adjectives before they view the sequence.

Free answers, suitable for group or class discussion.

4   Letter to a friend

This task can be used as a follow-up activity for homework to revise the past tense forms studied in Units 4 and 5.

5   Discussion

Students should keep a note of their opinions to refer back to later.

LANGUAGE STUDY

This section assumes that the students know the basic rules of forming comparatives and superlatives by adding –er and –est, or more and most.

Here is additional information which the class might find useful.

Formation

Adjectives formed with suffixes take the *more/most* forms:

beauty:	beautiful	more beautiful	most beautiful
hope:	hopeless	more hopeless	most hopeless
love:	loveable	more loveable	most loveable
content:	contented	more contented	most contented

Virtually all monosyllabic adjectives take the endings –er and –est.

Two syllable adjectives which take the endings –er or –est include those which end in –le, –ow, or –y:

little, littler, littlest

narrow, narrower, narrowest

happy, happier, happiest

Comparing one with many, and one with one

The ordinary form of many adjectives has in fact a comparative meaning. If we say *Joe is a tall man* then we mean that Joe is taller than the normal height you would expect if there were a large group of men: the comparison is not with any one person, but with the expected norm of a large group.

If we want to compare one person with another, then the specific comparative form is necessary:

Joe is taller than Prodip. Prodip is taller than Ted.

The next stage is to compare one with a known group:

Joe is the tallest of the three.

Marked adjectives

Consider these two questions:

A How far is it?

B How near is it?

In **A** the answer can range from very far indeed to extremely near. In **B** the questioner already expects that the answer will include 'near' and not 'far': the question is, *how* near?
The adjective 'near' is marked: it limits the range of answers by showing an expectation. The adjective 'far' is unmarked: the whole range of answers is possible.

Here is a list of common opposites, with the marked one first. Jumble the list, so that the students need to match the pairs before deciding which is marked and which is unmarked. (The context is important.)

near/far;   blunt/sharp;   short/tall;   low/high;   small/big;
narrow/wide;   little/much;   bad/good

1 It's as simple as ABC!

Exercise 1

The answers are:

as bold as brass	as green as grass
as cool as a cucumber	as keen as mustard
as deaf as a doorpost	as quick as a flash
as drunk as a lord	as quiet as a mouse
as dull as ditchwater	as sober as a judge
as fit as a fiddle	as strong as an ox
as free as a bird	as warm as toast
as good as gold	

Alliteration is a common feature of similes.

---

 5 Pronunciation

---

2 The sooner, the better

Exercise 2

Sample answers are:

A The earlier you go to bed, the more refreshed you feel in the morning.

B The more you eat, the fatter you get.

C The older you get, the wiser you become/get.

D The more money you have, the more you spend.

E The more you study English, the better you become.

F The less you exercise, the worse you feel.

---

 6 Drill

---

3 Fairly, slightly, or extremely?

Exercise 3

The answers are:
A 1) young   2) older, wiser   3) unmusical
B 1) weak   2) complicated
C 1) happy   2) sophisticated   3) worse
D 1) difficult   2) expensive   3) cheaper   4) cheap   5) good   6) bad   7) good
     8) more expensive, better   9) better, better   10) more expensive, richer

Exercise 4

⌣ = *similar meaning*

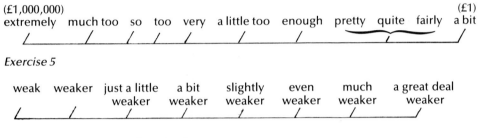

Exercise 6

Free answers suitable for group discussion.

91

UNIT 11

Hardly ever. Well, quite often.

Expressing frequency

AIMS

This unit marks the last third of the FOLLOW THROUGH course and in many ways is a consolidation unit.
The main focus is on two points of grammar: adverbs of frequency, and 'some and any'.

PRE-VIEWING PREPARATION

SIT COM: **1 Watching CONUNDRUM at the office**

DOC SPOTS: **Birds** reading passage and **1 Comprehension**
Public housing reading passage

CONUNDRUM: **1 Alec Lee – suspect**

LANGUAGE REVIEW

In this unit, you have consolidated your knowledge of

1 adverbs of time and frequency:
Never, hardly ever. Well, every now and then.

2 adverbial phrases of frequency:
three times a week   twice a day   every year   every other day

3 adverbial clauses of frequency:
I go to the theatre whenever there's a good play on.

4 the use of *some* and *any*:
positive sentences – *I've got some money.*
questions – *Have you got any money?*
negative sentences – *I haven't got any money.*
informal requests – *Have you got some money?*

5 and you have practised admitting that you've done something wrong, or telling someone that they've done something wrong:
I shouldn't have spent so much money on holiday.
You should have come with me.

KEY WORDS AND PHRASES

accommodation
to acccuse (someone of
   something)
an acquaintance
agricultural

ALWAYS
frequently
often
generally
normally
usually

anyhow
authority
a bank account
to breed
boring
a chunk
a colleague
to consider
in the course of
to go deaf
to deliver newspapers
desperate
to drain
a dreamer
a doughnut
dull
evidence
an exception
   to make an exception
fault
   It's not my fault!
to fine
frustrated
generous
a habitat
a horizon
a human being

HOUSING
private accommodation
public housing
People usually live in flats,
bungalows or houses;
bureaucrats refer to 'dwellings'
and 'units'.

a marsh
matter
   What's the matter?
to migrate
migration
to mix up
a mix-up
a mood
   to be in a good/bad mood

NEVER
hardly ever
rarely
scarcely

nourishing
an offence
   to commit an offence
a representative
a reserve
to respect

SOMETIMES
now and then
once or twice
occasionally

a species

RUBBISH
Rubbish is the general term for
things we do not want. **Litter** is
paper scattered on the street or
in a park. **Waste paper** is paper
that has been used usually in
offices. Bins and baskets are
used for rubbish: **rubbish bins,
litter bins,** and **waste-paper
baskets. Dustbins** are for
household rubbish (American
English = **'trash can'**).
Stuff is used only in spoken
English: 'Do you like that stuff?'
It means something worthless.

talented
a television series
a temper
   to be in a (bad) temper
   to lose one's temper
unfair

UNFAIR DISMISSAL
to dismiss someone
to give someone the sack
to sack someone
to be sacked
to fire someone
to be fired

AMERICAN ENGLISH
I guess so.
In America 'to guess' is used for
'to think' or 'to agree'.

▷ SIT COM

1 Watching CONUNDRUM at the office

A If the students do not know the adverbs listed, then run through them first. Otherwise play the scene twice through, asking the students to listen out for the adverbs of time.

The correct order is:

never, (scarcely ever)/hardly ever, occasionally/every now and then, sometimes, quite often, often, (frequently), (normally), always
(words in brackets = answers to **2 In the park**)

B Prepare the list of nouns with the students and then show the sequence again. Note that the students may find it difficult to get the direction of the effect of the adjectives correct. Thus 'surprised' is needed, and not 'surprising' and 'contemptuous' is wanted to describe Ted, rather than 'contemptible'.

This is the complete list of correct and inappropriate answers: surprised/surprising; annoyed/annoying; defensive/defensible; contemptuous/contemptible; humiliated/humiliating; amazed/amazing; furious/infuriating; frustrated/frustrating. The adjectives nervous, angry, resentful and indignant do not have corresponding adjectives with a force in the opposite direction.

2 In the park

This is an extension of **1A**. The answers are included in brackets above.

3 In the canteen

Notice the power that somebody such as Mrs Belmont has over Ted Stenhouse. Use this as an extra discussion point with the class. Is this normal or unexpected? What similar situations do the students know from their experience?

4 Billy's letter

If the students need it, use the pause button to focus attention on Billy's actions. Notice how he gradually moves from being cheery to sensing that something is wrong.

The letter is suitable for private study or for homework.

D◉ DOC SPOT 1   Birds

1 Comprehension

Present the text and comprehension questions as standard, and then watch the sequence.
The answers are:
A 1)   **B** 1)   **C** 1)   **D** 2)   **E** 2)

1   Listen for detail

2 That's wrong!

With some classes, the students can be split into groups of three: **A**, **B**, **C**. In each group, **C** is the most able student. **A** reads the question from the book; **B** answers the question from the book. However, **C** is not allowed to look at the book, and must correct the answer from memory.

Possible answers are:

A   No, it isn't. It's in Kent.

B   No, less than that. About one hundred and twenty species visit the reserve.

C   No, during the winter there may be twenty thousand widgeon in the area.

D   No, the natural marsh grasses and rushes provide all the food the birds need.

E   No, it was being drained for agricultural purposes.

3   Initials

Note that items **A – F** are pronounced as groups of letters: R – S – P – C – A
(are-ess-pee-see-ay) and so on. Items **G – L** are pronounced as words:
UNO = youknow; UNESCO = younessko; WHO = who; UNICEF = youneeseff;
NATO = naytoe; and UEFA = you-ay-fa

The answers are:

A   The Royal Society for the Prevention of Cruelty to Animals

B   The Automobile Association

C   The Amateur Athletics Association

D   The British Broadcasting Corporation

E   The British Boxing Board of Control

F   The Independent Broadcasting Authority

G   The United Nations Organisation

H   The United Nations Educational, Scientific and Cultural Organisation

I   The World Health Organisation

J   The United Nations Children's Fund

K   The North Atlantic Treaty Organisation

L   The Union of European Football Associations

4   Bird talk

A   The early bird catches the worm. = If you get up or arrive early then you will be successful.

B   A bird in the hand is worth two in the bush. = Something that you have definitely got is better than something you haven't yet got, but hope to get.

C   Two swallows do not make a summer. = An early or isolated occurrence should not be taken as the general rule.

D   Birds of a feather flock together. = Similar types of people tend to meet and/or like each other, eg teachers meet teachers, policemen meet policemen, and so on.

E   Kill two birds with one stone. = to incidentally achieve two things when attempting to achieve only one; to solve two problems at once

> a *swansong* is the last piece of work or performance of a writer, artist, actor, etc
>
> a *birdie* in golfing terms means that the golfer takes one stroke fewer than is average for a particular hole, i.e. is *one below par* (par = average)
>
> a *duck* in cricket terms is when a batter is caught or bowled out before he/she has scored any runs (*out for nought*)
>
> a *bird's-eye-view* is a view seen from high up, as a bird in flight would see

In classes with the same mother tongue, invite translations of these (and other) proverbs.
With mixed classes, invite the students to translate their own proverbs into English, so that other students who speak a different language can guess what they mean.

D DOC SPOT 2   Public housing

Prepare the text as standard, and then show the sequence.

1   Comprehension

Use the comprehension exercise as a follow-up task, explaining the meanings of the distractors in each example.

The answers are:

A 3)   **B** 2)   **C** 1)   **D** 3)   **E** 1)

2   Praise and criticism

There are many acceptable answers. When the students give their answers they may vary in their degree of criticism. This variation can be exploited in a similar way to Sit Com **1 Watching CONUNDRUM in the office**. For example, the first prompt may elicit these sentences:

1) There's no light at all.
2) There's not much light.
3) It's not true that there's plenty of light.
4) There's hardly any light.

Ask the students to sort out the degrees of how much light there is.
Answer = 1), 4), 2), 3).

3   A letter

Preparation in pairs can be followed up as individual study for homework.

4   The perfect house

This can be turned into a small project – the outcome of the discussions can be presented in writing; plans, drawings or models can be made. Or give the class a specific 'problem plan' to solve, eg plan a house for a family with 4 children, where the mother works from home so she needs a quiet office, the father needs a workshop to pursue his hobbies at the weekend, elderly grandparents who cannot climb stairs also live in the house, etc. Then take a vote on the best plan to solve all the problems.

◎ CONUNDRUM

1   Alec Lee – suspect

Check comprehension of the listed sentences before showing the scene, so that the students can follow the interrogation.

The answers are:

A √   **B** ×   **C** √   **D** ×   **E** √   **F** ×   **G** ×   **H** ×   **I** ×   **J** ×

2   Alec Lee and Bernie Raistrick

The students should know the adjectives listed by now.
Free answers, suitable for discussion in groups or as a class.

3   Discussion

Encourage the students to use their imagination. Perhaps somebody in the class might get the right answer: not that it is Raistrick who murdered Gibbs, but that he might be afraid for somebody else.

---

   2   Who said it?   and   3   Drill

LANGUAGE STUDY

1 Hardly ever. Well, quite often.

WS Gilbert and Arthur Sullivan created a light-hearted genre of satirical operetta, with works such as *H.M.S. Pinafore, The Pirates of Penzance,* and *The Mikado.* These works are frequently performed by amateurs.

Exercise 1

The students can add to the activities listed in the box, and make sentences using words and phrases of frequency studied in Sit Com **1 Watching CONUNDRUM in the office.**

Free answers.

2 Every morning, once a week

Exercise 2

The answers are:
A 5)   B 2)   C 1)   D 3)   E 4)

 4   Drill

3 When, whenever

Exercise 3

The answers are:
A 3)   B 5)   C 1)   D 4)   E 2)

4 Some or any?

The main rules may already be known to many students.

Exercise 4

This is suitable for oral work in class or for homework.

The answers/questions are:
A Are there any doughnuts today?
B Did we have any deliveries last week?
C Do we need any more doughnuts for next week?
D Are we expecting any deliveries next week?
E Have you reserved any doughnuts for Joe?

The example **B** *Oh, Joe, have you got some money on you?* is used in some circumstances in colloquial English where the speaker is not only asking for money, but is also expecting to be given money. The speaker is really saying: *Joe, lend me some money.* It could thus be used amongst very close friends, close colleagues or members of the same family. In less familiar circumstances, it would be considered impolite.

 5   Drill

5 Doing something wrong

This gives students revision in using the modal 'should' to tell someone they have done something wrong.

Exercise 5

Possible answers are:

A You should have filled up with petrol at the last filling station.

B You should have gone to the bank yesterday.

C You shouldn't have run so far.

D I'm sorry, I should have remembered.

E You should have followed the map I gave you.

---

 6 Drill

UNIT 12

That's all very well, but...

Expressing opinions, agreeing and disagreeing

AIMS The main aim of this unit is to extend the students' knowledge of English into more difficult registers, such as the language of political argument. The theme of this unit is followed up in Unit 13.

PRE-VIEWING PREPARATION

SIT COM: **1 Politics: the arguments**
4 In the office

DOC SPOTS: **The London Silver Vaults** reading passage and **1 Comprehension**
Marwell Zoological Park reading passage

CONUNDRUM: **1 Mrs Gibbs**

LANGUAGE REVIEW

In this unit you have practised

1 reporting what someone said or felt, using words like:
pointed out that. . ., argued that. . ., was sorry to say. . ., wondered if. . .

2 expressing your opinion:
As far as I can see. . .   *In my opinion. . .*
Well, if you ask me. . .   *As far as I'm concerned. . .*

3 agreeing with other people:
Exactly.
I quite agree.   *And I agree with you.*
You're quite right.   *That's what I think.*

4 disagreeing politely:
Maybe that's true, but. . .   *Well, yes, but don't you think that. . .*
That's all very well, but. . .   *Yes, but I'm not sure that I agree. . .*

5 embroidering an argument:
What I'm saying is. . .
Take starvation, for example. . .
But what do we do?

KEY WORDS AND PHRASES

absolutely
according to
an account
an accusation
an action group
an amount
an antique
art
an attitude
to balance
to blame
a border
to break a promise
brilliant
a campaign
    an election campaign
to come to power
to complain
an official complaint
a conclusion
to conduct
a consequence
to define
delicate
to destroy
destruction
to display (wares)
a district
economic affairs
to estimate
to fail
a figure (person)
    a leading figure
a figure (number)
    unemployment figures
foolish
frankly
a government
hypocritical
to ignore
an income

income and expenditure
inquisitive
intelligent
to interrupt
an interview
a lie
    to tell lies
a livelihood
to lose control
madness
a mayor
mysterious
nonsense
nowadays
to be in office
to organise
originally
overnight
to pass the time
a point
a politician
politics
power

PHRASES
As far as I'm concerned. . .
Whose fault is it?
It's your own fault.
Don't talk to me about (politics).
If I remember rightly. . .
I'm sick and tired of. . .
to run like a rabbit
to end up in prison
to protect someone's reputation
Politics is the art of the possible.
    (attributed to Otto von
    Bismarck, 1815–1898)
Anything for a quiet life.
I couldn't care less!

pressure
previously
a principle
    a matter of principle
a priority
a promise
    to make a promise
    to break a promise
to react
the real world
realistic
a reason
a reputation
research
    to do research
to resign
to respond to
a responsibility
to run out of
a scandal
secure
to solve
a species
starvation
storage space
suitable for
terrible
the Third World
a tourist attraction
a trader
unemployment
utterly
a vault
a vitamin
vitamin pills
a weapon
whole
wildlife
to be worth

SIT COM

1   Politics: the arguments

There are several ways of presenting this scene, one of which should be used only with students whose level of English is very good.

With most classes, prepare the viewing guide in advance, so that the students will be able to follow the difficult dialogue. Ask them what their opinions of the arguments are, and then play the scene. While watching, the students should note who uses which remark. In the subsequent discussion, there may well be differences of opinion about which arguments can be both pro and anti.

With classes at any level, it can be useful to play the scene with no preparation and also *without* the sound; the students must interpret what they see. Who is speaking to whom? Where? What about? . . . and so on. Then the guide should be prepared before playing the sequence with sound.

With very good classes, the scene could be shown with no preparation of the contents, just with a guided listening task. For example, how many arguments or objections can the class note for each speaker?

Possible answers are:

PRO = **A, C, G, H, I**   ANTI = **B, D, E, F**   EITHER = a matter of opinion!

On the whole the pro-government speaker refers to what he considers *practical*, whereas the anti-government speaker is more concerned with *principal*.

2   Politics: the manners

This exercise is intended to broaden the students' vocabulary. Play the scene again, and get the students to match the 'reporting' phrases with the gestures, behaviour and language of the two politicians. For the remaining words, or even all of them, the students could mine the phrases listed. Discovering the nuances of the different meanings could be a useful self-access task for some students.

1   Drill

3   In the restaurant

This exercise uses the language of **2 Politics: the manners** and reinforces the importance of sequence in using the past simple for narrative. It is suitable for private study or for homework.
The correct order is:
C, B, F, D, E, A (the order of **D** and **E** is debatable)

4   In the office

The viewing guide can be prepared before viewing the sequence, or watch the sequence once, prepare the guide and then show the sequence at least once again so that the students can complete the task successfully.
The answers are:

A Ted   **B** Ted   **C** Ted   **D** Ted   **E** Ted   **F** Sarah   **G** Sarah

Extend the task to reported speech by asking the class to tell you again what Sarah and Ted said or did, using the 'reporting' phrases learnt in **2 Politics: the manners**.

D🔘 DOC SPOT 1   The London Silver Vaults

1   Comprehension

Present the text and comprehension questions as standard and then show the sequence.

The answers are:

A 3)   **B** 1)   **C** 4)   **D** 5)   **E** 2)

2   Is this right?

This exercise encourages intensive reading.
Check answers against the reading passage.

[cassette icon]   2   True or false?

---

3   A newspaper article

This exercise can be extended to a full-scale project, with groups producing large scale 'wall' newspapers (including photographs and diagrams) for display in the classroom.

4   Silver talk

silver lining: 'Every cloud has a silver lining.' = Even bad news can contain an element of good news.

silver medal: a medal awarded to a person who comes second (between gold and bronze) in competitions, eg in athletics

silver screen: a nostalgic term for the cinema, recalling the great days of Hollywood

silver tongued: is used to describe people who can talk very fluently, especially confidence tricksters and politicians

silver wedding: is celebrated after 25 years of marriage.

Other wedding anniversaries are: pearl – 30 years; ruby – 40 years; golden – 50 years; diamond – 60 years. The terms *silver, gold*, etc are also used for the reigns of monarchs.
Queen Elizabeth II celebrated her Silver Jubilee in 1977; Queen Victoria celebrated her Diamond Jubilee in 1897.

Do the students know any similar expressions in their own language?

D🔘 DOC SPOT 2   Marwell Zoological Park

Present the text as standard, and then show the sequence.

1   Comprehension

Use the comprehension questions for follow-up work.
The answers are:

A ×   **B** √   **C** √   **D** ×   **E** √   **F** ×   **G** ×

[cassette icon]   3   Listen for detail

---

2 It is estimated that . . .

This exercise tests the students' ability to construct sentences with complicated syntax.

Some answers require a passive sentence. These transformations are admissable here, owing to the contents of the sentences. But remind the students that most passive sentences in English are not derived from a so-called corresponding active one.

Possible answers are:

A It is estimated that twenty-five per cent of all wildlife will become extinct within twenty years.

B Zoos have an important part to play in conservation.

C A world populated solely by human beings would be awful/unbearable for most of us.

D Most endangered species' main danger is man. (or) Most endangered species are threatened mainly by man.

E Affluent societies should be responsible for the preservation of endangered species.

3 Role play

This role play can be acted after the students have completed Language Study Exercises 1 and 2. The amount of preparation time needed will vary according to the capabilities of the students. In mixed ability classes, the less able students can participate in the final role play by reading set pieces, prepared with the help of others in the group.

4 Puzzle

The answer to **B** (rhino) can be given if the students' mother tongue word for this animal is completely different from the Greco-Latin stem.

The answers are:

A green	E nature	H affluent
B rhino	F preservation	I conservation
C extinct	G ecologist	J endangered
D evolution		

The key word is 'Greenpeace' – the name of an international environmental organisation which launched a campaign to protect the whale and is now concerned with the protection of other endangered species, including man.

5 Ecology and you

Some classes may wish to extend the discussion to take account of political and economic factors in the world-wide ecology debates. For example, Britain did not appear to worry about ecological questions during the time of the industrial revolution. Students could collect newspaper cuttings on ecological matters and use these as a basis for class discussion. Much of the vocabulary needed for this can be found in **Key words and phrases**.

 CONUNDRUM

1 Mrs Gibbs

The pre-viewing task is important, as it prepares the students for what Mrs Gibbs has to say and leads into Exercise 2.

Free answers, suitable for group or class discussion.

2   Mrs Gibbs' inverview with the police

Check if there are any surprises among the class about what Mrs Gibbs knows.
The answers are:
A √ B √ C √ D √ E × F × G ×

3   The bank manager

Students should compare their opinions and make a note of whose account they think Maxwell was enquiring about.

4   Bernie Raistrick

Get the class to consider the implications of this information. Why, for example, do the police not know this already? Who might have told them – but didn't?
The written task is suitable for homework.

LANGUAGE STUDY

1   That's all very well, but . . .

Ask students to read out the extract and to stress the words in italics. Students should learn and remember these ways of expressing opinions, agreeing and disagreeing.

2   In my opinion . . .

Point out that 'What I'm saying is . . .' would normally only be used to explain or to reinforce points that the speaker has already attempted to put across. The others can all be used to introduce an idea for the first time.

Exercise 1

Students can complete this exercise as an oral or written task in class. Any combination of answers is possible. Once **3 I agree/I disagree** has been completed, students can choose a topic from questions **A–E**, and in small groups conduct a role play where two students argue for the subject and two against.

3   I agree/I disagree

Stress that in certain circumstances it may be considered impolite in English to directly contradict someone.

Exercise 2

Possible answers are:
A In my opinion
B I quite agree
C as far as I'm concerned
D That's all very well, but
E what I'm saying is
F Maybe that's true, but
G If you ask me
H That's exactly what I think

---

   4   Pronunciation

---

4   Making a case

This exercise can serve as a useful introduction to skimming skills and reading for the main points of an argument.

The shortest summary is:

World problems could easily be solved if we got our priorities right.

5   Points of view

The writing task is suitable for homework. Students should choose between **A** and **B**. The task cards prepared by the groups themselves should reflect genuine issues of concern, as well as deliberately fanciful ones.

KEY WORDS AND PHRASES

5   Pronunciation

UNIT 13

I don't understand!

What to say when you don't understand

AIMS
This unit extends the students' ability to cope with language in more difficult registers. In particular, there is a focus on how to cope when you don't understand, and on gambits in conversations. Students will also learn a number of adverbs and adverb phrases to introduce a subject. This unit leads on from Unit 12.

PRE-VIEWING PREPARATION

SIT COM:
1 Psycholinguistics
2 At the university
3 The professor

DOC SPOTS:
Bath reading passage and **1 Comprehension** (optional)
The London School of Contemporary Dance reading passage

CONUNDRUM:
1 **Mrs Gibbs and the police**

LANGUAGE REVIEW

In this unit you have practised

1 What to say when you don't understand a word that someone uses:
I've just been to Moreton-in-Marsh.   *I went hang-gliding yesterday.*
You've just been where?   *You went what?*

2 some questions to ask when you don't understand a sentence:
Could you put it another way?
Could you give some examples?

3 a wide range of adverbs and adverb phrases to introduce something you want to say:
similarly, furthermore, likewise, there again, in short, etc.

4 some words and phrases which help to stress points, to summarise or to make an argument clear:
in other words, whereas, one could argue that, etc.
and some 'gambits':
to be honest, anyway, like I said, look

106

KEY WORDS AND PHRASES

to accompany
an achievement

an architect
to arrange
an aspect
an attitude
a background
background information
a believer
a brother-in-law
choreography
competence
to constrain
contemporary
creative
to go deaf
a decision
to delineate
to design
a development
    the latest developments
to be due
elegant
an excavation
an expert
a façade
fascinating
formerly

handwriting
harmony
a hobby
hot springs
instead
intricate
an individual
to be keen on
language
    bad language (cursing,
    swearing)
the lead role
to leave (to bequeath)

LINGUISTICS
Linguistics is the study of language, and how it works.
Applied linguistics helps with books such as this one.
Psycholinguistics is about the psychology of language.
Sociolinguistics is about how we behave and the language we use.

naive
to obey
to operate
a parameter

pollution
to precede
a professor
satisfaction
sophisticated
a spa town
a spectacle
stonework
to sum up
a technique

THINKING THOUGHTS
We **think** and **have thoughts.**
One thought might **inspire** us.
Thought is the abstract concept.

to trick
to trick someone into doing
    something
a union
a unity
unlocked
to volunteer

PHRASES
to put one's foot down
to a certain extent
to take notes
he left me a great deal of money
As far as I'm concerned . . .
to get a job done
It's a challenge!

▷ SIT COM

1 Psycholinguistics

The term *psycholinguistics* is explained for the students in the **Key words and phrases**.

The answer is: Billy

This is Billy's first assignment. Ask the students what they think this might mean for Billy's future career at FOLLOW THROUGH.

2 At the university

Run through the list of alternatives before showing the sequence. This list allows the students to talk about Billy's nervousness. Use mime to illustrate the meanings, or ask the students to mime the alternatives.

Check answers against the video, then discuss what the students do when they feel nervous.

3 The professor

Prepare the text in outline only, so that the students recognise what it is that Billy is supposed to be noting.
After the students have finished the task, replay the scene and use the freeze frame to focus attention on what Billy has written.
In fact, Billy has not made a note of anything the professor said, he has just scribbled on the paper. This type of aimless scribble that often turns into drawings or patterns is called *doodling*, from the verb *to doodle*.

4 In the office

Exaggeration, and often mild insults, are a normal part of conversation among English speakers who know each other well.

The answers are:

A Ted   B Ted   C Joe   D Ted   E Ted

---

1 Drill   and   2 Drill

D◉ DOC SPOT 1   Bath

Prepare the text as standard, then show the sequence.

1 Comprehension

These questions can be taught as pre-viewing preparation, or they can be used for follow-up work.

Sample answers are:

A in the county of Avon in the west of England

B It is famous for its Georgian architecture and its Roman remains.

C John Wood (1705–1754) was the architect who began the plans for the centre of Bath.

D No, it was not.

E The buildings are made of Bath stone.

F No, some modern buildings have been constructed which disrupt the harmony.

G an intricate system of Roman hot baths and swimming pools, and even an underfloor heating system.

H Hot springs are places where hot water comes naturally out of the ground.

2   Change the sentences

This activity requires intensive reading in order to find matching phrases.
The answers are:

A   entirely different
B   in a revolutionary way
C   the unity of design
D   under attack
E   set the fashion for (a whole generation of young people)

3   Famous for what?

The answers are:

A   In Spain, Pamplona is famous for its running bulls.
B   In France, Le Mans is famous for its 24-hour car race.
C   In France, Lourdes is famous for its holy water.
D   In Italy, Pisa is famous for its leaning tower.
E   In Italy, Venice is famous for its canals.
F   In the USA, New Orleans is famous for its Mardi Gras.
G   In the USA, San Francisco is famous for its bridge.
H   In Brazil, Rio de Janeiro is famous for its carnival.
I   In Greece, Delphi is famous for its amphitheatre.
J   In Scotland, Edinburgh is famous for its castle.

Extend this activity to famous places or sights in the students' own region or
country, in preparation for 5 **Attractive towns and you**.

4   Puzzle

The answers are:

A   plans
B   Queen's
C   Roman
D   pollution

E   Square
F   John
G   Wood
H   Somerset

The Pump Room in Bath is the room where people took supposedly health-giving
spa waters from a hand-pump. The Pump Room is still open to the public for
refreshments.

The abolition of counties and the creation of new ones, or the removal of county
boundaries, causes some people great upset, yet is unnoticed by others. Ask the
students whether the name of the area where they live means anything to them.

5   Attractive towns and you

This can be developed into full-scale project work, ending in the preparation of
brochures and wall-poster displays such as those in travel agents.

D⊙DOC SPOT 2   The London School of Contemporary Dance

Prepare the text as standard and then show the sequence.

1   Comprehension

Use the comprehension questions for follow-up work.

The answers are:

A major, main

B unusual, rare

C forget about

D considers

E difficulty

NB Tai Chi is a slow movement dance from the Far East. It is sometimes taught as a form of self defence.

2   An interview

This exercise provides the students with an opportunity to formulate questions. Extend the activity by transferring the dialogues to a well-known local institute of arts which the class can talk about.

Sample answers are:

Interviewer: What is this school called?

Interviewer: What course does it offer students who want to become dancers?

Interviewer: And do all your students find places in dance companies once they have completed the course?

Interviewer: Does the school only teach dance?

Interviewer: What do you think the students get out of the course?

3   Discussion

This discussion can be extended to take in the training of doctors, engineers, teachers, computer scientists, and so on. In the UK for example, there is a great surplus of people with university qualifications in arts subjects, such as history, but a shortage of graduates in mathematics.

CONUNDRUM

1   Mrs Gibbs and the police

Prepare the viewing guide with the students first, so that they have the vocabulary necessary to describe Mrs Gibbs' reactions.

Follow up **4 Bernie Raistrick** from Episode 12 – who could have told the police about Raistrick?

Answers: Students select suitable adjectives.

2   Bernie Raistrick and the police

The completed form should read:

Raistrick lied about the time he spent with Lee, and gave Lee a false alibi. He is convinced that Lee did not shoot his brother-in-law. He admits that Lee was worried about the video business, but he strongly denies being involved in the video business himself. He claims to be rich, as his father left him a lot of money a few months ago.

Follow the task with a discussion about Raistrick's possible involvement in the murder.

3   A motive: money

Ask the students if they think this is the only motive or can they think of any other motives for the murder of Matthew Gibbs?

LANGUAGE STUDY

1 I don't understand!

This studies a formal, academic register of language which many students at this level may find daunting. It suggests practical ways of coping with difficult words and sentence structures, and gives students practice in demystifying complex structures.

With academic subjects, it is difficult to avoid specialist vocabulary. But in ordinary speech and writing, simpler words can often be found. Note that using too many words from Latin or Greek roots in non-specialist texts will often make the language sound very formal and even artificial or stilted.

Exercise 1

The correct answers/questions are:

A You went *what* (last Saturday)?
B You went *what* (yesterday)?
   (dirt-track racing = a form of motor-cycle racing)
C You've just bought a new *what*?
   (put-you-up = a chair or sofa which can be turned into a bed)
D The prettiest place you know is *where*?
   (Moreton-in-Marsh = a small town in the Cotswolds)
E He was wearing a really *what* suit? (natty = smart)
F *Who* was the first to use *what* (on road surfaces)?
   (John Laudon McAdam, 1756–1836)

Point out to the students that the words in italics should be stressed and uttered with a rising intonation: You think it's *what*?

4 Drill

Exercise 2

Possible answers are:

to advise	= to tell	to assist	= to help
to commence	= to start	to discontinue	= to stop
to desist	= to stop	to implement	= to carry out
to proceed	= to go ahead	to inform	= to tell
to utilise	= to use	to purchase	= to buy

Exercise 3

Students compose their own answers. This exercise is suitable for homework or private study.

5 Pronunciation and intonation

Exercise 4

Sample summary:

Language may not necessarily precede thought, but the level of linguistic competence does limit an individual's thinking.

This statement could be used as a basis for group discussion.

2 Adverbs and adverb phrases

This provides students with a wide range of adverbs and adverb phrases to introduce something they want to say.

Exercise 5

The answers are:

A moreover, furthermore

B there again, nevertheless
(at the same time)

C likewise, similarly

D that is, in particular

E first, next

F after all, at the same time
(nevertheless)

G hence, therefore

H since then, lately

I in short, in conclusion

3 Like I said

This switches attention to a different register of language and focuses on colloquial ways of introducing remarks.

Exercise 6

The answers are:

A (4)   B (3)   C (1)   D (2)

UNIT 14

You should see a doctor!

Giving advice and dealing with personal matters

AIMS

The focus in this unit is on interpersonal language, including gestures and behaviour, as well as spoken words. Showing attitudes and indicating relationships have been covered in earlier units, but this is the first time that these aspects of phatic communion are brought together systematically.

PRE-VIEWING PREPARATION

SIT COM: **1 In the canteen**

DOC SPOTS: **Citizens Advice Bureau** reading passage and **1 Comprehension**
The Victoria and Albert Museum reading passage

CONUNDRUM: **1 Alec Lee's alibi**

LANGUAGE REVIEW

In this unit you have studied the type of English that is used when dealing with personal matters, relating to other people or to yourself. In particular, you have practised

1 paying compliments:
   That looks lovely.

2 expressing sympathy:
   I am sorry to hear that.

3 giving advice:
   You should see a doctor.
   You ought to see a doctor.

4 what to say when you are being defensive:
   You may think I'm being hard, but I'm not.
   or when you have changed your mind about something:
   Perhaps it won't be necessary to. . .
   Can we just forget the whole thing?

KEY WORDS AND PHRASES

absolutely
absurd
an accusation
to make an accusation
advice
to allow
to be allowed to
apart from
to bet
to blame
a branch
a brute
brutish
a bureau
certain
change (money)
a citizen
a cleaner
a client
to deal with
decorative
decorative arts
definitely
definitely not
a departure lounge
a designer
to disappear
dishonesty
distress
to be in distress
either. . .or. . .
elderly
an enquiry
to enter
entire
to be entitled to
evidence
fair
to be fair
favourite
to fund

TO GET

to get on with someone = to be friendly with someone

to get on with something = to start or to continue working

to get something out of someone = to make someone give you information, or money, or a promise

to get round to something = to start working on something you've been meaning to do for a long time

a grant
to handle
initial
to investigate
a leaflet
a local council
lovely
a majority
to manage
to manage to do something
marriage guidance
a message
a milkman
necessary
nowadays
an opinion
originally
to owe
partly
to pour

PROBLEMS

to have a problem

to pose a problem

to solve a problem

proof
a query
to refer to
to reassure
the said wallet
a service
a solicitor
to steal
supplementary benefit
to support (oneself) financially
to tolerate
tolerance
   intolerance
training
to trust (someone)
unfair
useful
a vegetable
a vegetable garden
a wallet
to waste
to water
a welfare state

PHRASES
I've been having trouble with . . .
to tell you the truth . . .
I'm afraid . . .
as soon as possible (=asap)
One has to draw a line somewhere.
You're far too kind!
You know . . .
Let me get this straight.
not a lot
a minute or two
up and down the country

SIT COM

1 In the canteen

Prepare the guide with the students before showing the sequence. The students must appreciate the interplay between Ted and Mrs Belmont. In subsequent scenes, Ted's reactions are even more obvious.

The answers are:

Mrs Belmont **B** √   Ted **C** √

2 In the office

Note Corinne's use of mild insults, exaggeration and ridicule. This is acceptable language among people who know each other well.

The answers are:

A 3)   **B** 4)   **C** 1)   **D** 2)

3 In the park

This exercise in register follows on from Unit 13 and it concludes Billy's adventures with the park keeper.

Students should compose their own answers using official language for the park keeper's report and informal language for Billy's point of view.

4 The policewoman

When Billy enters, use the freeze frame for speculation about where Ted's wallet is.

Students' answers can be acted out.

Use the following vocabulary information as the basis for extra language work:

A thief thieves things from people. He commits theft.
A robber robs places, such as banks, eg a bank robbery.
A robber also robs people of things.
Both thieves and robbers steal things from people.
A robbery is usually on a much larger scale than a theft.
If something is stolen from you, then you report a theft or robbery.
Burglars break into houses to steal things.

D◉ DOC SPOT 1   Citizens Advice Bureau

1 Comprehension

Prepare the text and comprehension questions as standard. Once students understand the topic, play the sequence.

Note the use of the word *citizens*. According to strict rules of punctuation, it should be followed by an apostrophe: *citizens'*. This indicates the relationship, ie an advice bureau that belongs to the citizens (as in *policeman's whistle*). However, there is a move towards using such nouns as qualifiers, as in *police whistle*.

In Britain, people who have been employed and then lose their job can claim unemployment benefit – regardless of how much money they have. The unemployment benefit (UB) is a type of insurance. Supplementary benefit is paid to people who need more money than UB, or who have never paid into the UB scheme.

There is a rock group called *UB 40:* that is the code number of the form on which the unemployed must claim.

The answers are:

A √   **B** √   **C** √   **D** ×   **E** √   **F** ×   **G** ×

1   Listen for detail

2   What else?

The word *else* is used to include any or all other possibilities. The question *'What else?'* is open: anything can be listed, although the situation, or common sense, might impose limits.
Compare the use of *else* in these words:
Who else?   Where else?   What else?   How else?
with the use of *–ever* in:
Whoever . . .?   Wherever . . .?   Whatever . . .?   However . . .?
The *–ever* words indicate one specific answer within the complete range that is available.

Whatever can I do? means 'I want to do one thing, chosen from many.'

What else can I do? means that a variety of things, (or just one thing) could be chosen from many possibilities.

The answers are:

A   There must be something else I can do, but I don't know what.
B   Can't you play your trumpet somewhere else?
C   There isn't anywhere else I can go! (or) There's nowhere else I can go!
D   It wasn't me! It must have been someone else.
E   We can go now. There's nothing else for us to do.
F   You must have taken it. No one else has the key to that room.
G   I only have these clothes to wear. Everything else is in the wash.
H   Why haven't we got a TV. Everyone else has (got) one.

2   Drill

3   I've got a problem

Let the students decide whether the problems should be real or imaginary.

4   Discussion

Extend the discussion to consider what government or private help there is for people in difficulty in the students' own country. In Britain, apart from unemployment benefit (UB) and supplementary benefit (SB) there is also Family Income Supplement (FIS) paid by the Department of Health and Social Security (DHSS). This is only given to very needy families. The DHSS also pays sickness benefit to working people who must stop work because they are ill.

D◉ DOC SPOT 2   The Victoria and Albert Museum

Prepare the text as standard. Once students understand the topic, play the sequence.

1   Comprehension

With good classes, ask the students to identify the source of the distractors:

A   *reigned* looks like *resigned,* as implied in 2)
B   *art* is used to describe both paintings and sculpture
C   an enemy at war is a *rival*

D *customs* are what we do, and the people who wait at airports are *customs officials*

E guidebooks *cite* the best *sights* in London

The answers are:

A 3) **B** 3) **C** 1) **D** 2) **E**3)

2 As a result . . .

Questions **A, C, D** and **E** need the second argument putting first, as in the example. This exercise follows up Unit 9, which dealt with cause and effect, as well as giving practice in syntax.

The answers are:

A He left his fingerprints everywhere. As a result, the police were able to arrest him.

B The printers went on strike. As a result, no newspapers appeared today.

C I was in bed with flu. As a result, I didn't sit the exam.

D The government refused to increase the subsidy. As a result, the farmers stopped selling eggs.

E The two kings had an argument about a piece of land. As a result, the war broke out.

3   Drill

3   Is this the British Museum?

Extend this into a role-play for two, and then develop it further by applying the dialogue to local buildings and places well-known to the students.

Sample dialogue:

Tourist:	Excuse me.
You:	Yes, can I help you?
Tourist:	Is this the British Museum?
You:	I'm afraid not. It's the Victoria and Albert Museum.
Tourist:	Oh! My mistake. When was it built?
You:	It was built in the 1860s.
Tourist:	And what does it contain?
You:	Lots of things – furniture, ornaments, costumes, toys. It's the biggest museum in the country.
Tourist:	I see. By the way, who *are* Victoria and Albert?
You:	Not 'are', 'were'. Queen Victoria and her husband Prince Albert are dead.

4   Puzzle

The answers are:

A museum   **B** Albert   **C** white   **D** London   **E** We are not amused.

Kings and Queens may use 'we' when they mean 'I'. This is known as the 'Royal We'.
A groom in the royal household, the Honorable Alexander Grantham Yorke, imitated Queen Victoria. 'We are not amused,' was her reaction, written in her *Notebooks of a Spinster Lady,* 2nd January 1900. She was of course a widow, not a spinster.

5   King Edward VIII

King Edward VIII abdicated in 1936 so that he could marry Mrs Wallace Simpson, a divorced American citizen. After his abdication, he took the title of 'Duke of Windsor'.

The King's brother became King George VI; when he died in 1952, his daughter Princess Elizabeth took the throne as Queen Elizabeth II. Her heirs are Prince Charles and his elder son William.

 CONUNDRUM

As the mystery moves to a conclusion, the students will enjoy the dénouement and eagerly await the moment when the murderer is revealed in Unit 15. Episode 14 finishes with a surprising twist, without the solution being given. Exploit the opportunities for speculation and prediction throughout the episode.

1   Alec Lee's alibi

The flashbacks remind the students of the opening scenes in the hotel, when Gibbs was murdered.

The answers are:

1) **A**   2) **E**   3) **F**   4) **C**   5) **D**   6) **B**

The written table is suitable for private study or for homework.

2   Bernie Raistrick's flashback

The students may well be divided between Raistrick and Lee as the main suspects. Who could Raistrick have been calling?

The answers are:

B√   **D**√

3   Bernie Raistrick's alibi

This list of the cast can be used by the students for **5 Whodunnit?**

Students can discuss the answers as a class.

4   A telephone call

Phillips is talking to a policeman or policewoman, who is probably calling from the police station. He is going to the airport.

5   Whodunnit?

This is the time for the students, either individually or in groups, to commit themselves to a solution.

  4   Who said it?

LANGUAGE STUDY

1   You should see a doctor!

Students should observe the facial expressions of Ted and Mrs Belmont which reveal that Ted is trying to make a joke and Mrs Belmont is not amused.

Exercise 1

This should be an easy exercise. Its main aim is to prepare the students for Exercise 2.

The answers are:

A you should . . .
B I'm sorry to hear that . . .
C either that, or . . .

D How are you today?
E Lovely!

118

Exercise 2

Students can act out these sequences as role play, using the language and expressions observed in the video sequence.

2   You ought to . . .

Exercise 3

This exercise offers the students consolidation practice in giving advice based on their own work. It also makes explicit the link between *should* and *ought to* in this context, which may be needed by some students.

3   Ted's decision

Ensure that the students understand Ted's expressions before starting Exercise 4.

Exercise 4

Encourage each group to make up their own cue cards.

4   Shall we forget the whole thing?

Exercise 5

This can be turned into an extended role play.

   5   Pronunciation

UNIT 15

Family Fun or Follow Through?

Word stress and Consolidation

AIMS

This unit brings together various aspects of the course and therefore has a few special features:

* There is only one Doc Spot, which is about the role and influences of television.
* The FOLLOW THROUGH staff in the Sit Com find that their programme is going to be taken off the air.
* The 'Conundrum' serial ends and the murderer and motive are identified.
* The Language Study section picks up on several points from the whole course and also offers students some advice and rules about word stress.

As the students are likely to be keen to see this last episode, it may be advisable to deal with the material in the following way:

1) View the Sit Com and Doc Spot, up to the moment when Billy starts to watch 'Conundrum'.
2) Work through the Language Study.
3) Watch 'Conundrum' and the closing sequence of the Sit Com.

PRE-VIEWING PREPARATION

SIT COM: **1 In the street**
3 In the restaurant

DOC SPOT: **Television** reading passage

CONUNDRUM: **1 The language of money**

LANGUAGE REVIEW

In this unit you have consolidated your knowledge of English in a number of areas. You have

1 learnt some rules of stress connected with word endings:

engi'neer   *de'tective*   *phi'losophy*

and in noun phrases:

a 'plastic 'bag   *a 'quiz show*

2 studied officialese and verbosity and learnt how to use it or how to avoid using it:

in the not too distant future = soon

until such time as = until

3 studied useful adverbs and redundant adverbs:

It sounds quite good, actually.

quite unique = unique

4 practised some more adventurous ways to use adjectives:

There is a beautiful small young brown-speckled female wren nesting in our garden.

You have also discovered the solution to the 'Whodunnit?' in CONUNDRUM. When did you first suspect the murderer?

And finally, you have said goodbye to the FOLLOW THROUGH team, who will move on to Current Affairs. Except Billy, of course. He's off. . . I wonder where? Goodbye, Billy, and good luck!

And goodbye and good luck to all teachers and learners of English with FOLLOW THROUGH!

KEY WORDS
AND PHRASES

actually
an alternative
alternative
apparently
to attribute to
to belong to
to benefit
to bet
a commodity
to confess
to consult
cultural
a culture
to cure
current affairs
democracy
to depend on
dependence (independence)
to devastate
a diet
to disrupt
a drug

COMPOUND ADJECTIVES
strong-willed
absent-minded

enormous
expertise
a fantasy
frankly
to grab
an identity
an impact
inferior
an inheritance
an instrument
to involve
to be involved in
karate
a karate chop
a link
the mass media
a medium
a meeting
a memo (memorandum)

MONEY MATTERS
a bank account
a credit card
an inheritance
a will
a bank balance
an overdraft
to transfer money

naturally
odd
an offer
to offer
to panic
a paper clip
a pill
prestige

a quiz
recently
to receive
to replace something
a representative
to resign
a reward
rural
to shock
silly
a soap opera
a society
a solicitor
to spend (money or time)
technology

TELEVISION
TV
telly
the box
a television set

TEST LATEST!
A newspaper advertisement for
a test match of cricket.

a tendency
the Third World
Third World countries
a threat
a tool
a tranquilliser

▷ SIT COM

1   In the street

This exercise develops further the students' ability to talk about people's actions and behaviour. Prepare the guide before playing the video sequence.

The answers are:

BEFORE: **A, D, F**   AFTER: **D**

2   The suspect

The students have already had their attention drawn to the difficulties of accurate description. This guide can be used as the basis for a quiz-type contest between individuals or small groups. Do not prepare the guide with the students; show the sequence, and then ask for descriptions of the suspect.

3   In the restaurant

This is our last meeting with Pierre, the owner of the French restaurant. He leaves us with his typically tall tales.

The correct order is:

Pierre's uncle: **C, E, A, B, D, F**   Pierre's aunt: **G, C, D, A, E, B F, H**

Students can discuss what is true and what is an exaggeration.

4   At the bank

This can be prepared in advance, or used in the same way as **2 The suspect** above.

The writing task is suitable for homework or private study.

5   Who was who at FOLLOW THROUGH?

By now, the students should know the characters quite well and may have identified with them in some way. Compare the students' descriptions and discuss any differences of opinion.

An end-of-course celebration or party might be suitable in many classes. Also, students may want to discuss what they plan to do in the future.

D◉ DOC SPOT   Television

Prepare the text as standard, and then show the sequence.

1   Comprehension

Use the comprehension questions for follow-up work.

The answers are:

A stimulate   E expertise
B inferior   F colonialism
C prestige   G screen
D disrupt

2   I disagree!

This is an easy revision exercise, which is meant to encourage those students who have found parts of the course difficult. The activity can easily be extended to reported speech to make it more difficult.

Sample answers are:

A I disagree. I think (that) television is a poor educational medium.
B I disagree. I think (that) people are bored when they watch television.
C I disagree. I think (that) most American programmes are of good quality.

D I disagree. I think (that) political leaders introduce television for prestige.

E I disagree. I think (that) most Third World countries do have enough money to make programmes.

F I disagree. I think (that) television disrupts social ties in the West.

1 Pronunciation and 2 Listen for detail

3 Television programmes

There are four channels in the UK: BBC 1, BBC 2, ITV and Channel 4. There are also regional variations, for example on Channel 4 and BBC 1 some programmes are broadcast in Welsh to Wales. ITV and Channel 4 are funded by advertising (not sponsorship). The BBC is funded by a licence fee, collected annually from the owners of television sets.

Discuss with the class the methods of TV finance and control in their country.

BBC 1	BBC 2	ITV	CHANNEL 4
5.40 **Sixty Minutes** begins with news read by Moira Stuart at **5.40:** followed by weather at **5.55:** regional news magazines at **6.00:** and ending with news headlines at **6.38.** 6.40 **Rolf Harris Cartoon Time.** 7.10 **Manimal.** Professor Jonathan Chase, the criminologist with the ability to change into the likeness of any animal he chooses, is on the trail of a smuggling ring headed by an unscrupulous diplomat. Starring Simon MacCorkindale (Ceefax titles page 170). 7.55 **Points of View.** Barry Took with another selection of viewers' letters. 8.10 **Panorama: a Vote for Europe?** A debate on the European election issues (see Choice). 9.00 **A Party European Election Broadcast** on behalf of the Labour Party. 9.10 **News** with John Humphrys. 9.40 **Film: The Blue Knight** (1973) starring William Holden and Lee Remick. Holden plays 'Bumper' Morgan, a dedicated but unorthodox Los Angeles policeman who finds himself increasingly at odds with his young superiors. This is an abridged version of a made-for-television film that ran for four hours and which won Emmies for Holden and the director, Robert Butler (Ceefax titles page 170).	5.35 **News** summary with subtitles. 5.40 **Film: Who's Zoo in Africa?** An RKO comedy starring James Finlayson and Dot Granger. 6.00 **Film: The Last Safari** (1967) starring Stewart Granger and Kas Garas. Granger plays Miles Gilchrist, a white hunter acting as guide to wealthy, pampered playboy, Casey. When the obnoxious Casey gets too much for Gilchrist, the guide leaves the safari to go and settle an old score with a killer elephant. Directed by Henry Hathaway. 7.45 **Vegetarian Kitchen.** Sarah Brown presents the second programme of her series and illustrates what can be done with the wide range of pulses available. Her guest is Claudia Roden who prepares a Moroccan bean soup. 8.10 **The Two Ronnies.** Messrs Barker and Corbett plus guests Stephanie Lawrence and Madge Hindle (r). 9.00 **A Party European Election Broadcast** on behalf of the Labour Party. 9.10 **Call My Bluff.** Robert Robinson chairs the witty word game between Frank Muir's team of Clare Francis and Patrick Lichfield and Arthur Marshall's comprising Lynsey de Paul and Robin Bailey (r).	5.45 **News** 6.00 Thames news. 6.25 **Help!** Viv Taylor Gee with news of the success of the Broadwater Farm Estate, the once notorious housing estate in Tottenham. 6.35 **Crossroads.** John Latchford is on the wrong end of Kath Brownlow's tongue. 7.00 **What's My Line?** Odd occupations to be guessed from a brief mime by Ernie Wise, Jilly Cooper, Patrick Mower, Barbara Kelly and George Gale. 7.30 **Coronation Street.** Curly Watts informs the Rovers' regulars that he has seen a UFO (Oracle titles page 170). 8.00 **Brass.** The gorgeously funny send-up continues with Bradley and Prudence Makepeace getting into more hilarious situations. 8.30 **World in Action.** An examination of Britain's shipbuilding industry, now responsible for less than one per cent of tonnage launched in the world. 9.00 **European Party Election Broadcast** on behalf of the Labour Party. 9.10 **The Sweeney.** Regan and Carter investigate a hit and run killing. Was it by accident or by design? (r). 10.10 **News.** 10.40 **Des O'Connor Now!** Live music and chat from the Royalty Theatre, London.	5.30 **Jeopardy.** Another edition of the back-to-front quiz game presented by Derek Hobson. 6.00 **The Kellogg's BMX Championship** presented by Mick Brown, from Hounslow, to the west of London. The first in a six week series of team competitions involving professional riders from both sides of the Atlantic. 6.30 **Numbers at Work.** Fred Harris continues his invaluable series dealing with everyday mathematical problems with a look at measuring and decimals. 7.00 **Channel Four News.** 7.50 **Comment.** With a personal view on a matter of topical importance is Frances Stewart, a fellow in economics at Somerville College, Oxford. 8.00 **Scully.** Alan Bleasdale's Liverpool urchin in another escapade with his mate Mooey. 8.30 **Man About the House.** Comedy series. This week the rent money disappears and Jo fears that she may have to sell something she was keeping in her bottom drawer if she is unable to obtain an overdraft from the bank. 9.00 **Africa.** The sixth programme of Basil Davidson's eight-part history of Africa tells of the colonisation of Africa and the Africans' reactions to the settlers.

4 Puzzle

The answers are:

A nose	**E** list	**I** noise
B love	**F** Nile	**J** Elvis
C vile	**G** vote	
D slot	**H** solve	

5 Debate

Organise two speakers in favour of the motion, and two against. Give them a couple of days to prepare and practise what they want to say, and make sure the rest of the class is ready to take notes and ask questions.

The students can use all the rhetorical tricks and language of politics and debate that they have learned, especially the language taught in the last five units.

 CONUNDRUM

It may be preferable to deal with the Language Study material before viewing 'Conundrum'.

Whodunnit? Some students may have guessed the identity of the murderer – but it is unlikely that they will have guessed the motive correctly.

1 The language of money

Prepare this with the class before watching the last episode.
The answers are:
A 7) **B** 1) **C** 6) **D** 5) **E** 2) **F** 3) **G** 8) **H** 4)

2 Bernie Raistrick

Is it him? Discuss the motives he might have before watching the last scenes.

3 Michael Kelly returns

Or could it have been Kelly all the time? Ask the students to speculate on why he was trying to leave the country before they learn the real reason.

4 The solution

All is revealed: motive, method and opportunity.
Whodunnit? It's, or at least, it was, a conundrum.

LANGUAGE STUDY

1 Family Fun

Exercise 1

This exercise focuses the students' attention on the different endings that have been taken into English from other languages.

The endings *-ity, -ette, -esque, -ion, -eer, -ique, -ic, -ive* are from Latin or old French.

The endings *-cracy, -graphy, -logy,* and *-sophy* are from Greek.

---

 3 Word stress

---

2 Officialese and 3 Verbosity

Officialese and verbosity are commonly found in government documents. In the UK, there is great pressure on government departments – and on banks, insurance firms, and other institutions – to simplify the English that they use. There is a 'Campaign for Plain English,' which gives annual awards for clearly written English and condemns difficult English. Language which is hard to understand is known as gobbledygook ['gɔbəldi'guːk].

Here are the instructions for the Gobbledygook Test, which can be used to test the complexity of any passages in English. Use this with your students as a group activity.

1) Find a sample of writing 100 words long.
2) Count the number of complete sentences in the sample.
   This number is **S** in the formula.
3) Count the total number of words in all the sentences.
   The number of words is **W** in the formula.

4) Find the average number of words per sentence by dividing **W** by **S**.

The average is **A** in the formula: $\dfrac{W}{S} = A$

5) Count the number of words in the whole sample which have 3 syllables or more. This figure for the number of Long words is called **L** in the formula.

6) Add the Average **A** to the Long word figure **L** to get the final score: the difficulty rating (**D**).

For example:

100 words contains 12 sentences, with 5 words left over: **S** = 12.

The number of words in the sentences is 100 − 5 = 95: **W** = 95.

$$\frac{W}{S} = \frac{95}{12} = 7.9$$

The number of words in the whole sample with three or more syllables is 22:

L = 22.

A + **L** = 7.9 + 22 = 29.9

The difficulty rating for this sample passage is 29.9: **D** = 29.9

Call this first rating **D1**. Take more 100 word samples from the same text and obtain **D2**, **D3** and so on. Add these sample scores together, and divide by the number of samples to get the average. The final score is **F**. In formula terms, we have

$$F = \frac{D1 + D2 + D3 \ldots Dn}{n} \qquad D = A + L \qquad A = \frac{W}{S}$$

The difficulty rating **F** is also called, humourously, the Fog Index. Fog literally obscures our vision; in writing it obscures the meaning.

In the UK a Fog Index of 30 in a text represents the reading capability of the average 16 year old.

The most popular daily newspapers, such as *The Sun* and *The Mirror,* have a Fog Index of 26–28. *The Times* has a Fog Index of 36, and *The Guardian* of 39. Parts of legal forms can have a Fog Index of 100, or even more.

Exercise 2

The answers are:

A 4)   **B** 3)   **C** 5)   **D** 2)   **E** 1)

Exercise 3

Possible answers are:

A regarding	**E** concerning
B if	**F** until
C to	**G** regarding
D although	**H** considering

4   Stress

Exercise 4

Let the students prepare their answers before listening to the audiocassette, so that they can then compare their expectations with what they hear.

Some students may need help in hearing the different stress patterns in the phrases. With these students, play the audiocassette three times and ask the students to listen carefully for the stress. Only when they can hear the differences on repeated occasions should you ask them to repeat the phrases themselves.

Another way of explaining composite nouns is to consider them as similar to idioms. An idiom such as 'to pull someone's leg' is meaningless unless the whole phrase is spoken, and unless one knows the meaning (to tease, make jokes with somebody). If the phrase is interrupted, or the meaning of the idiom is not known, then the words must be taken literally.

It is the same with composite nouns. A 'blackbird' means something different from a 'black bird'. Often the composite noun has no connection with the components, eg a 'bluebottle' is a large flying insect, not a coloured bottle.

 4   Pronunciation and stress

5   Adverbs: useful and wasted

Exercise 5

This language study section reinforces some of the points made in earlier units. Remind the students that the inclusion of redundant adverbs in a sentence usually leads to a higher register of formality or politeness.

6   Adjectives   and   7   Adjectives as fantasy

Exercises 6 and 7

This section revises and extends the students' knowledge of adjective word order in English (see Unit 1). It also offers the student an open-ended opportunity for imaginative writing.

KEY WORDS AND PHRASES

Point out to students the different meanings of 'to hand something to someone':
Hand me that book, please. = Pass me that book, please.
and '(to have) to hand it to someone' (to admit someone's success):
You have to hand it to him, he's clever = You have to admit that he's clever.

 5   Pronunciation

Audio Scripts

UNIT 1

1   Welcome to FOLLOW THROUGH

Listen.
Good morning, Mrs Belmont.
Oh, hello, Billy. How are you today?
Fine, thanks.

Here are the names of some of the people in
FOLLOW THROUGH. Repeat the names and
point to the pictures in your book.

*Mrs Belmont, Billy Barker, Joe Ralston, Corinne
Roberts, Sarah Ashton, Pierre, Prodip Chopra,
Ted Stenhouse.*

2   Drill

What are they wearing?
Make questions about the clothes listed in your
book using:

'Who is it who . . .?'

For example, you hear:

a yellow pullover and a yellow bow tie

And you say:

*Who is it who is wearing a yellow pullover and a
yellow bow tie?*

Now you try.

a yellow pullover and a yellow bow tie
*Who is it who is wearing a yellow pullover and a
yellow bow tie?*

a green overall and brown trousers
*Who is it who is wearing a green overall and
brown trousers?*

a grey suit and a patterned tie
*Who is it who is wearing a grey suit and a
patterned tie?*

a lilac pullover and jeans
*Who is it who is wearing a lilac pullover and
jeans?*

a pink cardigan and a flowery dress
*Who is it who is wearing a pink cardigan and a
flowery dress?*

a grey pullover and an open-necked shirt
*Who is it who is wearing a grey pullover and an
open-necked shirt?*

a red skirt and brown boots
*Who is it who is wearing a red skirt and brown
boots?*

3   Listen for detail

The Purser is greeting passengers on a cross-
Channel ferry. Note down the words for all the
people who work on the ferry and the facilities
which are available.

Purser: Ladies and gentlemen, the captain,
officers and crew are pleased to welcome you
on board and wish you a pleasant voyage. The
following facilities are at your service: Bureau
de Change, hot and cold meals, perfumes,
cosmetics and souvenirs. If you have any
problems, please visit the Purser Information
Office.

4   Who said it?

Here are some of the people you'll see in
'Conundrum'.

Repeat their names.

*Michael Kelly, Alec Lee, Maurice Hutchinson,
Matthew Gibbs, Detective Chief Inspector Derek
Phillips, Detective Constable Jane Maxwell, Jenny
Gibbs, Bernie Raistrick, Felicity Curran*

Now, can you remember who said the following
in Episode 1?

If you're sure you don't mind.
Felicity Curran

When are you off again?
Bernie Raistrick

Tomorrow evening at nineteen thirty. To Tunis.
Alec Lee

I started last week, sir.
Michael Kelly

I thought you had to put your full address on
these things.
Detective Constable Maxwell

No tickets, no passport, no wallet. Nothing!
Detective Chief Inspector Phillips

5   Pronunciation and intonation

Repeat these greetings, using the same
pronunciation and intonation.

How do you do, Chief Inspector?

Hi, Billy.

How are things, Sarah?

Fine, thanks.

*Good morning, Mrs Belmont. How are you
today?*

Not too bad.

Good morning, Corinne. How's it going?

All right, thanks.

Good evening, sir.

Good evening.

Good afternoon, Constable.

6   Pronunciation

Listen and repeat:

There is one nice tall American television reporter on the FOLLOW THROUGH team.

Sarah sometimes wears her brown leather boots and her new red velvet skirt.

In 'Conundrum', Detective Constable Maxwell has to investigate her first murder mystery.

The cross-Channel ferry crews listen to regular BBC weather forecasts.

Pierre is very proud of his popular French restaurant.

UNIT 2

1   Corinne's plants

Listen to the advice that the gardener gave to Corinne:

No. No, I don't think more water will help it. Water it lightly, say about once a week during the autumn and winter, and you shouldn't have any problems.

I'm going to keep them nice and dry and warm till the spring and then I'll plant them out, in March or April.

You know the main thing a plant needs is love. Oh, and conversation, of course. Love and conversation. Oh, yes, I talk to them about all kinds of things. They like it.

2   Listen for detail

One of the Hampton Court gardeners is talking to Sarah about the maze. Note down the details.

Sarah: The one thing everyone knows about Hampton Court is the maze. When was the maze planted?

Gardener: Well, we think about 1690, approximately. There is evidence to suggest that some form of maze may have been there before, but the geometric construction, as it is today, well, it was probably constructed in the

1690s. You see, it takes up about a third of an acre in extent, and the paths within the maze are half a mile.

3   Drill

One of the visitors to Hampton Court says: We haven't done St Paul's yet, but we will. Make similar sentences. For example, you hear:

phone her

And you say:

I haven't phoned her yet, but I will.

Now you try.

phone her
I haven't phoned her yet, but I will.

read anything by Dickens
I haven't read anything by Dickens yet, but I will.

learn to drive
I haven't learnt to drive yet, but I will.

listen to that record.
I haven't listened to that record yet, but I will.

buy a new shirt
I haven't bought a new shirt yet, but I will.

go to that new restaurant
I haven't been to that new restaurant yet, but I will.

4   Drill

What does Billy plan for the future? What do you think he would say about the following? Remember, he plans to do a lot!

Make sentences, for example,

You hear:

Leave my job

And you say:

I'm going to leave my job.

Now you try.

Leave my job
I'm going to leave my job.

become a detective
I'm going to become a detective.

be a pop star
I'm going to be a pop star.

make television programmes
I'm going to make television programmes.

travel all over the world
I'm going to travel all over the world.

be rich and famous
I'm going to be rich and famous.

5 Pronunciation

Listen and repeat.

*breakfast; breakfast time; breakfast-time TV;
morning; morning coffee; coffee break;
afternoon; afternoon tea; tea time; tea break;
dinner; dinner time; supper; supper time;
lunch; lunch time; lunch hour*

UNIT 3

1 Listen for detail

Listen to what the expert on child behaviour says
and try to find the word for a baby who is just old
enough to walk.

Expert: So often a mother feels 'He's playing
quietly on his own. I can get on with my work',
and so she's not with her child. The result is
that the child very quickly becomes bored,
playing on his own, particularly if he's a
toddler. And mothers need to know that,
although they don't have to be doing
anything, they need to be with their child,
because this encourages him, whether he's
painting or whether he's making things or
whatever it may be.

2 Pronunciation

Repeat these words:

*chiropodist, gynaecologist, orthopaedist,
dermatologist, trichologist, paediatrician,
nutritionist, opthalmologist, gerontologist,
neurologist*

3 Listen for meaning

Here's a passenger talking about the
underground. Where does he live and why does
he need the underground in the evening?

Passenger: I'd like it to reach out a bit further
into the countryside, for a start. I live fairly
well out, up towards Epping, and the route out
there is very useful to us if we want to go into
the evening theatre or cinema. But it just
doesn't run late enough in that sort of area.
So, if it was to be improved in that direction,
obviously that's one of the things I would look
for.

4 Pronunciation

Repeat the names of these underground
stations:

*Oxford Circus, Green Park, South Kensington,
Sloane Square, Embankment, Westminster,
Notting Hill Gate, High Street Kensington*

5 Drill

Place orders in a restaurant. For example, you
hear:

We . . . a large bottle of mineral water.

And you say:

We'll have a large bottle of mineral water, please.

Now you try.

We . . . a large bottle of mineral water.
We'll have a large bottle of mineral water, please.

I . . . a glass of white wine.
I'll have a glass of white wine, please.

He . . . a glass of orange juice.
He'll have a glass of orange juice, please.

My wife . . . a tonic water.
My wife will have a tonic water, please.

We all . . . a salade Nicoise.
We'll all have a salade Nicoise, please.

6 Drill

Offer to do the following things. For example,
you hear:

I have to post this letter.

And you say:

I'll post it for you!

Now you try.

I have to post this letter.
I'll post it for you!

I have to water the plants.
I'll water them for you!

I have to make two phone calls.
I'll make them for you!

Then I'm going to feed the meter.
I'll feed it for you!

I haven't shut the window yet.
I'll shut it for you!

7 Pronunciation and intonation

Repeat these sentences:

I was going to see a film, but I saw a play instead.

I was going to drive, but I went by plane instead.

*I was going to have the Chicken Marengo, but I
had the beef instead.*

Don't mention it.

Fancy meeting you here!
He had something on his mind.

UNIT 4

1 Listen for detail

Where have the FOLLOW THROUGH staff been?

Can you remember who said what? Listen:

Do you know, I've never been abroad? Me, a man in my position – it's unthinkable, isn't it? Every year for the past five years I've gone to some boring English seaside town. But next year it'll be different. Next year it's going to be sunshine, beaches . . .

I went to Italy last year. Italy is really neat.

My family used to go to Tenerife every year. But I haven't been there since I was a child. I expect it's changed a lot since then.

I travelled all round North Africa and the Middle East when I was at University.

2 Listen for detail

Listen to this extract from the documentary on the Dickens Museum.

Note down the extra details which are not in the written summary.

Man: Dickens, because of his sudden rise in fortune and fame in the early 1830s, bought this as his first house, or rather leased it as his first house. He only lived there two years, but it is now the only surviving important house that Dickens lived in, in London. The Dickens Fellowship bought it in the 1920s and it's been opened as a Dickens Museum ever since. Consequently their collections are extremely rich and extremely interesting, and no other Dickens Museum could ever equal it in quality, though there are other small museums throughout Britain.

3 Pronunciation

Repeat the titles of Dickens' novels:

Oliver Twist, Nicholas Nickleby, Pickwick Papers, Bleak House, Little Dorrit, A Christmas Carol, The Old Curiosity Shop, David Copperfield, Great Expectations, Martin Chuzzlewit

4 Drill

Listen to the person's complaint and then give advice. For example, you hear:
I've got stomachache.
eat too much
And you say:
You've been eating too much.

Now you try.
I've got stomachache.
eat too much
You've been eating too much.

I'm always tired.
go to bed too late
You've been going to bed too late.

I'm too skinny.
not eat enough
You haven't been eating enough.

I'm too fat.
eat too much
You've been eating too much

I always lose at sport.
not train hard enough
You haven't been training hard enough.

I always fail exams.
not work enough
You haven't been working enough.

I'm always coughing.
smoke too much
You've been smoking too much.

5 Now, repeat these sentences:

I used to be fat, but I've been dieting and I'm not fat now.

I used to cough a lot, but I've been smoking less and I don't cough now.

I used to be skinny, but I've been eating more and I'm not skinny now.

I used to lose at sports, but I've been training hard and I don't lose now.

6 Drill

Make sentences about these people using 'used to'. For example, you hear:
Joe . . . live . . . America . . . England
And you say:
Joe used to live in America, but now he lives in England.

Now you try.
Joe . . . live . . . America . . . England
Joe used to live in America, but now he lives in England.

Prodip . . . work . . . India . . . London
Prodip used to work in India, but now he works in London.

Corinne . . . have . . . cat . . . plants
Corinne used to have a cat, but now she has plants.

Billy . . . be . . . schoolboy . . . officeboy
Billy used to be a schoolboy, but now he's an officeboy.

Mr Stenhouse . . . be . . . reporter . . . boss
Mr Stenhouse used to be a reporter, but now he's the boss.

UNIT 5

1 Drill

Make sentences from the words you hear using 'Tell us about . . .'. For example, you hear:
countries . . . visit

And you say:
Tell us about the countries you've visited.

Now you try.
countries . . . visit
Tell us about the countries you've visited.

people . . . meet
Tell us about the people you've met.

programmes . . . make
Tell us about the programmes you've made.

books . . . write
Tell us about the books you've written.

films . . . produce
Tell us about the films you've produced.

plays . . . direct
Tell us about the plays you've directed.

jobs . . . have
Tell us about the jobs you've had.

2 Listen for detail

Listen to this extract from the documentary on Whitstable oysters. The fisherman is talking about the cold winters of 1928/29 and 1947. What does he think killed the oysters?

Fisherman: Well, there I don't know what to put it down to. Some say with the disease now, you got trouble now with the oysters, and you can't put that down to weather. I mean, it's not like – being they're covered with water. This is

my theory. So if the water's over them and they're covered, you can't blame that for coldness. Only where there's very, very shallow ground.

3 Drill

Listen to these sentences and then repeat them.

Ogie has lived in Whitstable all his life.
Ogie lived in Whitstable all his life.
We used to row out to the fishing smack.
We're used to rowing out to the fishing smack.
We'd work for six hours.
We'd worked for six hours.
They are protected from bad weather.
They are protected by bad weather.

4 Drill

Make sentences to say what you have or haven't done, for example, you hear:
baseball . . . basketball (play)

And you say:
I've played baseball but I haven't played basketball.

Now you try.
baseball . . . basketball (play)
I've played baseball but I haven't played basketball.

Great Expectations . . . Martin Chuzzlewit (read)
I've read Great Expectations but I haven't read Martin Chuzzlewit.

Volkswagen . . . Ferrari (drive)
I've driven a Volkswagen but I haven't driven a Ferrari.

horse . . . camel (ride)
I've ridden a horse but I haven't ridden a camel.

Roast beef and Yorkshire pudding . . . steak and kidney pie (eat)
I've eaten roast beef and Yorkshire pudding but I haven't eaten steak and kidney pie.

And now a difficult one. Repeat the correct answer after you hear it.
London . . . Bristol (go to)
I've been to London but I haven't been to Bristol.

5 Pronunciation

Repeat the following:
I was wondering . . .
I'd really like to . . .
I was hoping that you'd . . .
That'd be great.
Sure.

UNIT 6

1 Listen for detail

Listen to Sarah talking to the stable girl in the documentary on training racehorses. As you listen, find words which mean . . .

'to clean out the horses' stables'
and
'riding equipment'
and
'low hills covered with grass'.

Now listen.

Sarah: How early do you have to get up in the morning?

Stable girl: About six. We come in; we check the horses have eaten up; you muck them out; and then you get your tack on, and you take them out; you bring them up to the downs, and you work them. You take them back; they get fed; then you have your breakfast, and then you come out and do it all over again till you're finished.

2 Listen and repeat

In the documentary on children talking, Sarah was surprised at one girl's answer to her question.
Listen:

What would you buy if you had a million pounds?
I'd buy some grapes.
A million pounds' worth of grapes?!

Now repeat the following responses, using the same intonation.

A hundred pounds' worth of tea?!
Ten dollars' worth of apples?!
Five pounds' worth of sweets?!
A million pounds' worth of grapes?!

3 Drill

Practise asking conditional questions using the words given. For example, you hear:
win a lot of money

And you say:
What would you do if you won a lot of money?

Now you try.
win a lot of money
What would you do if you won a lot of money?

meet Princess Diana
What would you do if you met Princess Diana?

see a bank robbery
What would you do if you saw a bank robbery?

find a wallet
What would you do if you found a wallet?

drop a ring in the river
What would you do if you dropped a ring in the river?

a friend breaks his arm
What would you do if a friend broke his arm?

hear a burglar during the night
What would you do if you heard a burglar during the night?

someone offers you a job in China
What would you do if someone offered you a job in China?

go bald
What would you do if you went bald?

4 Drill   Offering help

Before you practise offering help, repeat these verbs and make sure you know what they mean.

take the photograph
light the cigarette
dial the telephone number
feed the meter
post the letter
do the exercise
water the plant

Now you offer help, using the construction 'If you . . . I'll . . .' and the words given. For example, you hear:
camera/take photograph

And you say:
If you give me the camera, I'll take the photograph for you.

Now you try.
camera/take photograph
If you give me the camera, I'll take the photograph for you.

match/light cigarette
If you give me the match, I'll light the cigarette for you.

telephone number/dial it
If you give me the telephone number, I'll dial it for you.

money/feed meter
If you give me the money, I'll feed the meter for you.

letter/post it
If you give me the letter, I'll post it for you.

5   Drill

Listen to these sentences, then make new sentences using 'unless'. For example, you hear:
We'll go swimming if it's not too cold.

And you say:
We'll go swimming unless it's too cold.

Now you try.
We'll go swimming if it's not too cold.
We'll go swimming unless it's too cold.

We'll go for a walk if it doesn't rain.
We'll go for a walk unless it rains.

Your plants will die if you don't water them.
Your plants will die unless you water them.

I can't take a photograph if I don't have a camera.
I can't take a photograph unless I have a camera.

6   Pronunciation

Repeat these words:

PHOtograph, phoTOgrapher, phoTOgraphy, photoGRAphic
techNOlogy, technoLOgical, techNOlogist

UNIT 7

1   Listening comprehension

Listen to this extract from the documentary on electricity. The Senior Control Engineer is talking about one day's demand for electricity. As you listen, note down the times of greatest demand, the peaks, and the times of least demand, the troughs.

Senior Control Engineer: The peak of the day will be at half past five this evening when it gets dark. It'll be a very high peak because it's very wintry weather outside at the moment, and tomorrow, if the same conditions apply, we shall probably get the peak of the year, because it's colder than normal. We've got blizzards in the Midlands and the North and Scotland at the moment, even though it's only raining here, all of which produce a lot of load. After the evening peak, it just goes down all through the evening. We then have, er, TV pick-ups on the popular programmes that end around nine o'clock at night, ten o'clock at night, which may just give a slight jump in the demand curve, depending on the popularity, which we've got to work out ourselves beforehand. And then it just runs down until one o'clock in the morning and we have the off-peak storage heating that comes on. Everybody tries to use cheap electricity if they can. This will lift the load up again at that point for a little while and then it will run down to the minimum at about five, five-thirty in the morning, and start coming up again for breakfast.

2   Drill

Decide whether the following conditions increase or decrease demand for electricity. For example, you hear:
darkness

You say:
Darkness increases the demand for electricity.

Now you try.
darkness
Darkness increases the demand for electricity.

summer
Summer decreases the demand for electricity.

wintry weather
Wintry weather increases the demand for electricity.

blizzards
Blizzards increase the demand for electricity.

warm weather
Warm weather decreases the demand for electricity.

breakfast time
Breakfast time increases the demand for electricity.

3   Who said it?

Listen to these sentences spoken by characters in Episode 7 of 'Conundrum'. Can you remember who said them? Repeat them in reported speech. For example, you hear:
Lee has an alibi.

You say:
Phillips said Lee had an alibi.

Now you try.
Lee has an alibi.
Phillips said Lee had an alibi.

It's too late to put him in prison.
Mrs Gibbs said it was too late to put him in prison.

We want to catch his murderer.
Phillips said they wanted to catch his murderer.

Maybe there was an argument over money.
Maxwell said maybe there had been an argument over money.

There's something I'd like to show you.
Mrs Taylor said there was something she'd like to show them.

Raistrick is landing in an hour.
Maxwell said Raistrick was landing in an hour.

4 Drill

Listen to these sentences. If the sentence begins:
It's not as if . . .
You say:
At least . . .
And if the sentence begins:
At least . . .
You say:
It's not as if . . .
For example, you hear:
It's not as if parking here is against the law.
And you say:
At least parking here isn't against the law.

Now you try.
It's not as if parking here is against the law.
At least parking here isn't against the law.

At least it's not illegal.
It's not as if it's illegal.

It's not as if it's an offence.
At least it isn't an offence.

At least I'm not committing a crime.
It's not as if I'm committing a crime.

5 Drill

Rephrase these statements using either 'must have' or 'might have'. For example, you hear:
It's possible that she's been to Germany.
And you say:
She might have been to Germany.

Now you try.
It's possible that she's been to Germany.
She might have been to Germany.

I'm sure he's read that book.
He must have read that book.

I'm certain he's given up smoking.
He must have given up smoking.

I'm not sure whether they've gone to the cinema.
They might have gone to the cinema.

No, I'm sure they've gone swimming.
No, they must have gone swimming.

I think she was telling the truth, but I'm not sure.
She might have been telling the truth.

Perhaps Mrs Gibbs murdered him. It's possible.
Mrs Gibbs might have murdered him.

I'm certain it was an accident.
It must have been an accident.

6 Pronunciation

Repeat these words.

video recorder, videocassette, video piracy, video recording, fish and chips, pots and pans, boiling water

Now repeat these sentences.
Er, I bought a whatsit.
Er, I saw a thingummy-bob.
Er, I want a thingamajig.
Er, have you got a doo-dah?
What's-his-name told me.
And I told what's-her-name.

UNIT 8

1 Drill

Answer these questions about the Sit Com, then repeat the answer. For example, you hear:
Had Sarah been invited out to lunch by her boss before?
And you say:
No, she hadn't.
Then you hear the correct answer and you repeat it.

Now you try.
Had Sarah been invited out to lunch by her boss before?
No, she hadn't.

Was this the first time Ted had been to Pierre's restaurant?
No, it wasn't.

What had Ted been told about Sarah?
He'd been told that she was very fond of Italy.

Has Mr Smith agreed that Sarah can go to Italy?
Yes, he has.

Is Ted pleased with himself?
Yes, he is.

2 Listening comprehension

Joe is talking to a language student at the Polytechnic of the South Bank about learning with computers. The student gives a very long answer; but the most important part of his answer could be expressed in just two words.

Listen to the question and the answer, then decide what these two words are.

Joe: So how does this computer help you learn to speak a language?

Student: Well, this game is designed in various stages so that you can play it at various speeds. I play it at the slowest one, and there's constant repetition in the words that are used, the animals, the different actions you can take, and this constant repetition is really what drives into your mind, I hope for all time, the words that are used in the package.

3 Read and reply

Look at the timetable in your book and answer these questions.

Is there an Italian Advanced class at 6 on Wednesday?
No, there isn't.

Is there a French Advanced class at 9 on Wednesday?
Yes, there is.

Is there a German Beginners class at 8 on Friday?
Yes, there is.

Is there a Spanish Advanced class at 8 on Monday?
No, there isn't.

Is there a German Intermediate class at 7 on Wednesday?
Yes, there is.

Is there a French Beginners class at 7 on Monday?
No, there isn't.

Is there a Spanish Intermediate class at 9 on Monday?
Yes, there is.

4 Drill

These sentences are from the documentary on acid rain, but one word or phrase is missing from each sentence. Repeat the sentences with the missing words or phrases. For example, you hear:

What have these places got (. . .) common?
And you say:
What have these places got in common?

Now you try.
What have these places got (. . .) common?
What have these places got in common?

They are all threatened (. . .) acid rain.
They are all threatened by acid rain.

Sulphuric acid falls back to earth (. . .) lakes and (. . .) trees.
Sulphuric acid falls back to earth into lakes and onto trees.

It can travel (. . .) Scandinavia.
It can travel as far as Scandinavia.

Large areas of forest consist only (. . .) dead trees.
Large areas of forest consist only of dead trees.

Is there anything that can be done (. . .) acid rain?
Is there anything that can be done about acid rain?

Filters can prevent the acid getting (. . .) (. . .) the air.
Filters can prevent the acid getting out into the air.

5 Drill

Now practise some ways to describe feelings using the word 'by'. Change the sentences you hear like this. You hear:

That play was amusing.

And you say:
I was amused by that play.

Now you try.
That play was amusing.
I was amused by that play.

The book was fascinating.
I was fascinated by the book.

The film was impressive.
I was impressed by the film.

The actor was boring.
I was bored by the actor.

The actress was amazing.
I was amazed by the actress.

UNIT 9

1 Drill

Repeat these apologies; make them sound sarcastic.

I'm so sorry I interrupted you.
I'm so sorry I woke you.
I'm so sorry I startled you.
I'm so sorry I surprised you.
I'm so sorry I made you angry.
I'm so sorry I made you late.
I'm so sorry I upset you.

2 Drill

Repeat these sentences from the documentary on Mount St Helens, adding the missing words. For example, you hear:

In May 1980, a volcano (. . .) in the state of Washington.

And you say:

In May 1980, a volcano erupted in the state of Washington.

Now you try.

In May 1980, a volcano (. . .) in the state of Washington.
In May 1980, a volcano erupted in the state of Washington.

For scientists, it was an (. . .) opportunity to study the effects of volcanoes.
For scientists, it was an unprecedented opportunity to study the effects of volcanoes.

The earth below gets colder and the effect of (. . .) is suppressed.
The earth below gets colder and the effect of convection is suppressed.

There are (. . .) in some places and (. . .) in others.
There are droughts in some places and floods in others.

The more eruptions there are, the colder and more (. . .) the weather is.
The more eruptions there are, the colder and more erratic the weather is.

3 Drill

According to Dr John Gribbin, many things are 'due to' volcanic eruptions. Make sentences with 'due to' about the following. For example, you hear:

clouds of dust and ash

And you say:

Clouds of dust and ash are due to volcanic eruptions.

Now you try.

clouds of dust and ash
Clouds of dust and ash are due to volcanic eruptions.

some droughts and floods
Some droughts and floods are due to volcanic eruptions.

some fires and rainstorms
Some fires and rainstorms are due to volcanic eruptions.

some cold and erratic weather
Some cold and erratic weather is due to volcanic eruptions.

4 Drill

Maxwell doesn't believe what Raistrick says.

Repeat these sentences.
He says he was a friend of a friend.
He says he was in the hotel having dinner.
He says he had coffee in the lobby.
He says they were together for every minute.
He says he can't tell us anything.

5 Pronunciation

Repeat these sentences.
I'm late because the train was delayed.
He's ill. Consequently, he won't be coming.
His bed was very uncomfortable. As a result, he didn't sleep all night.
I didn't play football, owing to my bad leg.
Shall we start dinner without them, since they're late?
Mary can't walk very easily as a result of an accident.

6 Drill

Use the very polite phrase 'Would you mind . . .?'

to ask people to do things. For example, you hear:
work late
And you say:
Would you mind working late?

Now you try:
work late
Would you mind working late?

close the window
Would you mind closing the window?

open the door
Would you mind opening the door?

help me with this
Would you mind helping me with this?

come to work earlier
Would you mind coming to work earlier?

make less noise
Would you mind making less noise?

UNIT 10

1 Stress

The same words can mean different things depending on stress. Listen:

She's quite _young_.
The speaker means she _is_ young.

She's _quite_ young.
The speaker means she's _not_ very young.

Repeat these sentences, then decide what the speaker means.

It's quite cold.
Is it cold?
Yes, it is.

It was a fairly good film.
Was it a good film?
Yes, it was.

I thought it was quite a good meal.
Was it really a good meal?
No, it wasn't.

He quite liked her.
Did he like her a lot?
No, he didn't.

It was fairly good.
Was it good?
Yes, it was.

2 Drill

A tea taster is comparing teas. Repeat these sentences, adding the missing words. They are all comparatives or superlatives. For example, you hear:

The world's (. . .) tea producers are India, China and Sri Lanka.

And you say:
The world's largest tea producers are India, China and Sri Lanka.

Now you try.
The world's (. . .) tea producers are India, China and Sri Lanka.
The world's largest tea producers are India, China and Sri Lanka.

The worlds (. . .) importer of tea is Great Britain.
The world's biggest importer of tea is Great Britain.

The taster can see whether their performance is (. . .) or (. . .) than previously.
The taster can see whether their performance is better or worse than previously.

Tea which grows fast produces (. . .) flavour than tea which grows slowly.
Tea which grows fast produces worse flavour than tea which grows slowly.

3 Listen for detail

In the documentary on tea, the tea taster mentions the importance of altitude and which part of the tea bush is plucked. Now listen and note down the details.

Tea taster: And the tea, for example, that grows a 6,000 or 7,000 feet in equatorial Africa or in Ceylon, produces a certain flavour, possibly because of the coolness of the climate or the elevation itself, which is not available on tea which is grown in a lower elevation.
Prodip: What part of the bush do you use?
Tea taster: You take the most succulent part, which is the shoot at the top, the bud and the leaves on either side of it, and – these pluck very easily – they're very brittle and very juicy, and this produces the best flavour. Those people who have less stringent rules about plucking will go lower into the bush, and they will diminish the quality of the tea as a result.

4 Drill

Listen to these sounds. What does each one sound like? Make sentences using: 'It sounds like a . . .'.

Here's an example:
(sound of violin)
And you say:
It sounds like a violin.

Now you try.
(sound of violin)
It sounds like a violin.

(sound of drum)
It sounds like a drum.

(sound of double bass)
It sounds like a double bass.

(sound of guitar)
It sounds like a guitar.

(sound of saxophone)
It sounds like a saxophone.

(sound of flute)
It sounds like a flute.

5 Pronunciation

Listen and repeat these similes:
as bold as brass
as cool as a cucumber
as deaf as a doorpost

as drunk as a lord
as dull as ditchwater
as fit as a fiddle
as free as a bird
as good as gold
as green as grass
as keen as mustard
as quick as a flash
as quiet as a mouse
as sober as a judge
as strong as an ox
as warm as toast

6 Drill

When Billy asks how soon Ted wants the film, he is told:
The sooner the better.

Reply to these questions in a similar way.

How early shall I come?
The earlier the better.

How big would you like them?
The bigger the better.

How long should they be?
The longer the better.

How high shall we have them?
The higher the better.

How late shall I stay?
The later the better.

How many do you want?
The more the better.

UNIT 11

1 Listen for detail

Sarah is talking to a man from the Elmley Marshes bird reserve. Note down the details.

Man: These marshes are a huge area at the mouth of two rivers, The Medway and the Thames, and for years they've been a haven for wetland birds, wild fowl and waders and so on, and, in recent years, machines have made it possible to drain these marshes for more profitable agricultural use, and a lot of the marshes were disappearing and the habitat which these birds need for their survival was disappearing fast, so we decided to come into this area to get quite a large part of it to protect for the birds here.

Sarah: Can you tell me how many species you have?

Man: Well, over the whole year, well over 100 species, perhaps 120 or 130 species, but it's in winter that huge populations occur, when things like the widgeon come in as winter visitors.

2 Who said it?

How well do you know Episode 11 of 'Conundrum'? Can you remember who said the following?
So we can't charge him.
He's wrong.
You told them! You idiot!
She's a lady; Felicity Curran.
I've told you once! I was with Raistrick.
And we know that Matthew Gibbs was a colleague, a business acquaintance of yours.
We've broken his alibi.
Let me remind you that we're talking about murder.

3 Drill

In Episode 11 of 'Conundrum', when Lee said . . .
I don't know anything about that!
. . . Phillips responded . . .
Then you'd better tell us what you do know about.

Respond to these statements in a similar way, with appropriate intonation.

I didn't see her!
Then you'd better tell us who you did see.

I haven't heard that!
Then you'd better tell us what you have heard.

I don't go there!
Then you'd better tell us where you do go.

I didn't say that!
Then you'd better tell us what you did say.

I didn't tell them!
Then you better tell us who you did tell.

4 Drill

Express the following phrases with adverbial phrases of frequency. For example, you hear:
on Mondays and Fridays
And you say:
twice a week

Now you try.
on Mondays and Fridays
twice a week

at eight o'clock, twelve o'clock and four o'clock
three times a day

once in the morning and once in the afternoon
twice a day

on Mondays and Thursdays
twice a week

from June to September every year
every summer

once in the spring and once in the autumn
twice a year, every spring and autumn

in January, March, May, July, September and November
every other month

5 Drill

Answer these questions with a positive or negative statement. For example, you hear:
Are there any buses to Liverpool today?
No.
And you say:
No, there aren't any.

Now you try.
Are there any buses to Liverpool today?
No.
No, there aren't any.

Is there any tea in the pot?
Yes.
Yes, there is some.

Are there any cream cakes?
No.
No, there aren't any.

Are there any tickets available for the play tonight?
Yes.
Yes, there are some.

Are there any seats in the front row?
No.
No, there aren't any.

6 Drill

Respond to these sentences with 'should have' or 'shouldn't have'. For example, you hear:
I locked the door.
And you say:
Well you shouldn't have locked the door.

Now you try. Always say that the speaker has done the wrong thing.
I locked the door.
Well you shouldn't have locked the door.

I didn't shut the window.
Well you should have shut the window.

I didn't post the letter.
Well you should have posted the letter.

I told Jean and Arthur.
Well you shouldn't have told Jean and Arthur.

I'm sorry. I wasn't thinking.
Well you should have been thinking.

UNIT 12

1 Drill

Look at the list of 'statement' verbs in your book. Starting with 'pointed out', use these verbs to report these statements that Prodip made. For example, you hear:
There's no need for starvation in the world.
And you say:
Prodip pointed out that there was no need for starvation in the world.

Now you try.
There's no need for starvation in the world.
Prodip pointed out that there was no need for starvation in the world.

There's enough food for everyone.
Prodip indicated that there was enough food for everyone.

It just needs organising.
Prodip made it quite clear that it just needed organising.

We spend money on weaons.
Prodip stressed that we spent money on weapons.

We destroy huge amounts of food every year.
Prodip emphasised that we destroyed huge amounts of food every year.

We keep prices high.
Prodip hinted that we kept prices high.

It's madness.
Prodip reminded us that it was madness.

That's not the point.
Prodip argued that that was not the point.

2 True or false?

Listen to these sentences. Some are from the passage about 'The London Silver Vaults' and some are from the paragraph 'Is this right?'

Are the statements true or false?

There are thirty corridors with three vaults in each one.
False.

They're all one hundred and twenty-six feet below Chancery Lane Underground Station.
False.

The Silver Vaults are in Chancery Lane, which is in London's legal district.
True.

There are three long corridors.
True.

Now the vaults are used by all kinds of dealers and traders.
False.

3   Listen for detail

Joe speaks to a man from Marwell Zoological Park. According to him, what can people do to help conservation? What would zoos like to do if they could afford it?

Joe: What can the average person do to protest against this?
Man: Well, I think voices raised in protest is terribly important, but also money is terribly important too and I think it's the duty of every person who can afford to, to provide some of their money for conservation of wild life either through the organisations concerned with trying to save species in the wild, or to organisations such as ours. We, like most zoos, are largely financed by people coming through the gates. However, to keep large breeding groups is not economic in those terms because the average visitor would be just as happy looking at two scimitar-horned oryx as he would be looking at this herd where there were ten cows born this year. So we're keeping all these additional animals because we have a bigger purpose than just attracting the public, and for that reason zoos that are running properly organised scientifically understood conservation programmes need financial support.

4   Pronunciation

Repeat these 'opinion' phrases:

As far as I can see . . .
In my opinion . . .
Well, if you ask me . . .
As far as I'm concerned . . .
I'd say that . . .
What I'm saying is . . .

Now repeat these expressions of agreement:
Exactly.
I agree with you.
I quite agree.
You're quite right.
That's exactly what I think.

And finally expressions of disagreement:
Maybe that's true, but . . .
That's all very well, but . . .
Well, yes, but don't you think that . . .
Yes, but I'm not sure that I quite agree . . .

5   Pronunciation

Listen to these words and phrases and then repeat them.

an action group
an election campaign
an official complaint
unemployment figures
income and expenditure
to make a promise
to break a promise
to end up in prison

UNIT 13

1   Drill

Listen to this example. You hear:
You think all women are stupid, don't you?
And you say:
No, not all women, just some.

Now you respond to these questions in a similar way:
You think all women are stupid, don't you?
No, not all women, just some.

You think all books are boring, don't you?
No, not all books, just some.

You think all jobs are dull, don't you?
No, not all jobs, just some.

You think all children are noisy, don't you?
No, not all children, just some.

You think all bosses are bad, don't you?
No, not all bosses, just some.

You think all office boys are lazy, don't you?
No, not all office boys, just some.

2 Drill

Listen to this example. You hear:
I'm a great believer in doing a job properly.
And you say:
So am I.

Now you try. Respond to these sentences in a similar way.
I'm a great believer in doing a job properly.
So am I.

I went to the cinema last night.
So did I.

I had seen the film before.
So had I.

And I want to see it again tonight.
So do I.

I've seen lots of films.
So have I.

And I'll see lots more.
So will I.

I like films very much.
So do I.

3 Listen for detail

Here is Sarah introducing her report on Bath. Note down the extra information, which is not in your book.

Sarah: Here, in 1725, the architect John Wood revealed plans for a new style of building, a style that later set the fashion for the whole of Britain. Wood wanted to create an unbroken architectural harmony in each building. His buildings look like palaces, but they're really groups of individual homes unified behind the elegant facades. Among John Wood's major achievements here in Bath, are Queen's Square, completed in 1736, and the Circus, in which the buildings form a great circle enclosing a park. This was the first design of its kind in England. The work begun by John Wood, was continued by other architects, including his son, and in the 1760s, work started on Royal Crescent, which many people see as the finest expression of the new style.

4 Drill

Listen to this example. You hear:
I'm going to see the Wojtaczeks tomorrow.
And you say:
You're going to see who?

Now you ask the right question using 'Who?', 'What?' or 'Where?' when you don't understand a word.
I'm going to see the Wojtaczeks tomorrow.
You're going to see who?

I went hang-gliding last Saturday.
You went what?

I went dirt-track racing yesterday.
You went what?

I've just bought a new put-you-up.
You've just bought a new what?

The prettiest place I know is Moreton-in-Marsh.
The prettiest place you know is where?

He was wearing a really natty suit.
He was wearing a really what suit?

McAdam was the first man to use tarmacadam on road surfaces.
Who was the first man to use what?

5 Pronunciation and intonation

Repeat these sentences:
I'm sorry, I don't understand.
Could you repeat that please?
Could you give some examples?
I'm not sure I know what you mean.
Could you put it another way?

UNIT 14

1 Listen for detail

Listen to this extract from the documentary on Citizens Advice Bureaux. The first-time visitor is talking to Kathy about her mother. As you listen, write down what Kathy asks and what she offers to do.

Kathy: Come in. Hello.
Visitor: Hello. I believe I have an appointment.
Kathy: How can I help you?
Visitor: Well, it's difficult really to know where to begin, but, there's a couple of things I'd like to ask your help on. The first thing is that my father died recently and my mother's been left living on her own. As you must realise, she's quite elderly.
Kathy: Well if you like, I'll make an appointment and she can come in to see us and I'll help her fill out the forms.
Visitor: Oh!
Kathy: Will that be any good?
Visitor: Yes, that would be very useful.

2 Drill

Listen to this example. You hear:
You can't play here.
And you say.
Play somewhere else.

Now you try. Rephrase these statements using the word 'else':
You can't play here.
Play somewhere else.

You can't have this.
Have something else.

You can't talk to him.
Talk to someone else.

You can't stand there
Stand somewhere else.

You can't buy that.
Buy something else.

You can't see her.
See someone else.

You can't park there.
Park somewhere else.

You can't take this.
Take something else.

You can't meet him.
Meet someone else.

3 Drill

Listen to this example. You hear:
He lost the papers because there was a hole in the bag.
And you say:
There was a hole in the bag. As a result, he lost the papers.

Now you change the following sentences using 'as a result':
He lost the papers because there was a hole in the bag.
There was a hole in the bag. As a result, he lost the papers.

The plants died because you didn't water them.
You didn't water the plants. As a result, they died.

Ted got a parking ticket because Billy forgot to feed the meter.
Billy forgot to feed the meter. As a result, Ted got a parking ticket.

Sarah couldn't do the report because she was busy.
Sarah was busy. As a result, she couldn't do the report.

4 Who said it?

Listen to these questions and answers from Episode 14 of 'Conundrum'. Can you remember who said what and to whom?
Repeat each sentence in reported speech.
Just tell us what happened.
Phillips told Lee to tell them what had happened.

After dinner Raistrick and I had coffee.
Lee replied that after dinner he and Raistrick had had coffee.

Did you see his gun when you were in his room?
Maxwell asked Lee if he had seen Gibbs' gun when he'd been in his room.

Where were you and what did you do between 7.45 and 8 o'clock?
Phillips asked Raistrick where he had been and what he had done between 7.45 and 8 o'clock.

Well, after Alec Lee went to see Gibbs, I talked to a young lady.
Raistrick replied that after Alec Lee had gone to see Gibbs, he had talked to a young lady.

5 Pronunciation

Repeat these sentences:
That looks lovely!
I am sorry to hear that.
You should see a doctor.
You ought to see a doctor.
I hate having to do it, but it may be necessary.
One has to draw a line somewhere, you know.
Of course, I know I'm partly to blame.
I've been far too kind.
. . . and now look what's happened.
You may think I'm being hard, but I'm not.
I can't be fairer than that, can I?
What else can I do?

UNIT 15

1 Pronunciation

Listen to these sentences and repeat them with the same stress and intonation.
I disagree. I think television is a poor educational medium.
I disagree. I think people are bored when they watch television.
I disagree. I think most American programmes are of good quality.
I disagree. I think political leaders introduce television for prestige.

I disagree. I think most Third World countries do have enough money to make programmes.
I disagree. I think that television disrupts social ties in the West.

2 Listen for detail

In the documentary on television, an expert on television in Sri Lanka gives details of how television has affected his country and of something that has happened partly as a result of it. Note down the details of what he says.

Expert: Our society in Sri Lanka is an agricultural society. It is a poor society, where 80% of its people live in its rural areas. Now, a characteristic of a rural society is strong kinship ties, communal ties, of the absence of what in this society may be called individualism. Now, the first consequence of the impact, or the first consequence of the introduction of television, has been a tendency for people to get away from their communal relationships and their cultural ties, to sit around the box and become individualised atoms. They first see a way of life, the consumption of goods and commodities that are totally unavailable to them. On the one hand, this has made the people very dissatisfied and set in process political demands which are not within the capacity of the government to grant. This has brought in its wake social tensions, political tensions, which, not having the opportunity to find expression in the normal process, has resulted in, has, I wouldn't say it has caused, it has been a primary cause, but it has contributed in a very large way to the holocaust that occurred in my country during the last two months when atrocities and social violence of a sort that we've never seen in our country before, occurred. Now I attribute, and not only I, many social scientists in my country attribute these social upheavals primarily, I would say, to the penetration of our society by television.

3 Word stress

Listen.

shampoo, philosophy, engineer, detective, bacteriology, investigation, technique, cigarette, geography, linguistic, administration, production, picturesque, democracy, familiarity

4 Pronunciation and stress

Listen and repeat.

quiz show, dining room, door knob, murder mystery, park keeper, Oxford Street

Family Fun, plastic bag, London taxi, Tuesday morning, back door, Detective Constable, Follow Through, Picadilly Circus

5 Pronunciation

Repeat these words.

actually, a commodity, a culture, cultural, dependence, independence, to disrupt, expertise, a karate chop, the mass media, prestige, a representative, rural, a solicitor, technology, a tendency, a tranquilliser, strong-willed, absent-minded, TV, telly, the box, a television set

Now repeat these phrases.
So what's new?
I bet you did!
She lived to a ripe old age.
He died of a broken heart.
What a waste of time!